BLUEBEARD'S CHAMBER

BLUEBEARD'S CHAMBER

Guilt and Confession in Thomas Mann

───────◆───────

MICHAEL MAAR

Translated by David Fernbach

VERSO
London • New York

This edition first published by Verso 2003
© Verso 2003
Translation © David Fernbach 2003
First published as *Das Blaubartzimmer: Thomas Mann und die Schuld*
© Suhrkamp Verlag 2000
All rights reserved

1 3 5 7 9 10 8 6 4 2

Verso
UK: 6 Meard Street, London W1F 0EG
US: 180 Varick Street, New York, NY 10014–4606
www.versobooks.com

ISBN 1–85984–529–0

British Library Cataloguing in Publication Data
A catalogue record for this book is available from the British Library

Library of Congress Cataloging-in-Publication Data
A catalog record for this book is available from the Library of Congress

Typeset in Perpetua by The Running Head Limited, Cambridge
www.therunninghead.com

Printed and bound in the US by R.R. Donnelley & Sons

CONTENTS

ROOM WITH DEAD CAT
1

'VOLUPTUOUSNESS AND HOT GUILT'
35

CREDEMI
91

Acknowledgement
107

Translator's note
109

Extract from *The German Republic*
113

Notes
117

CHAPTER ONE

ROOM WITH DEAD CAT

THERE WAS JUST one occasion when Thomas Mann's children found him in a state of despair. The maelstrom that swept Germany in 1933 overtook Mann while he was on an extended lecture tour abroad. When he began to suspect that he would be unable to return home, his first anxieties were for a number of notebooks, bound in oilcloth, that he had left locked in a Munich cabinet. These were his old diaries, which he feared might fall into the wrong hands. After weeks of growing disquiet, he forwarded to his son Golo, who was staying in Munich, the keys for the drawers and cupboards, explaining that he wanted the notebooks sent in a suitcase as freight to Lugano.[1] Golo recalls a further instruction:

'I am counting on you to be discreet and not read any of these things!' A warning I took so seriously that I locked myself into the room while I was packing the papers. When I came out with the suitcase to carry it to the station, there was faithful

Hans offering to take this bothersome chore off my hands. All the better, and why not?[2]

It was soon to emerge, however, that Golo's excess caution almost proved his father's undoing. By locking himself in his father's study, he drew the attention of the chauffeur – Hans Holzner, in fact a Nazi informer – to the fact that something secret was involved. Holzner did indeed take the suitcase to the station, but he also reported the matter to the political police.[3]

Thomas Mann was now faced with a torment of waiting. On 24 April he noted his disquiet over the suitcase's long delay; anxiety put out its first tentacles. Three days later the non-arrival of the case was already 'uncanny', and he slowly grasped that something was wrong. The following day his suspicion grew firmer: 'The chauffeur Hans, gradually revealed as a Judas.' On 30 April he woke up at five o'clock stricken with terrifying thoughts about the suitcase and the diaries. His outward demeanour began to suffer, as we know from the reports of his children. Golo describes how his father 'fell prey to growing impatience, finally even to despair'.[4] And Erika writes of this 'unprecedented state of excitement, indeed desperation', in which he found himself.

Finally, on 2 May, the all-clear arrived; the case was now on Swiss soil, probably in Lugano: 'Significant and deep relief. The sense of having escaped a great, even inexpressible, danger, which perhaps never existed at all.'[5]

A weighty word, this 'inexpressible', for a man who knew how to choose his words. And in her own account of those gloomy weeks, his daughter uses equally striking terms:

As it transpired to his relief, the overwhelming issue was the diaries, which he believed not only to be definitively lost, but to have fallen into the hands of a mortal foe. In their unfathomable stupidity, however, they soon released the suitcase quite intact, and T.M., now ready for flight and unwilling to risk a repetition of anything similar, burned a large number of papers at the first opportunity.[6] [. . .]

Were they 'compromising', these neat exercise books? They may well have been. No lifespan is free of a 'Bluebeard's chamber'.

Later on Erika tones this down somewhat, explaining that nothing offensive need have occurred. But the Bluebeard metaphor continues to resonate. The little anecdote with which she continues is again far from reassuring:

When [Hugo von] Hoffmannsthal first got to know T.M., still in his youth, he is said to have declared that the entire personal impression he received was of someone uncommonly well-groomed, with an upper-class solidity and discreet elegance. His home, too, gave the same appearance: very fine and spacious, with valuable carpets, dark oil paintings, club armchairs, bright sleeping quarters, etc. 'The only thing, though,' the poet continued, looking down at his fingernails – 'in a little side room there was suddenly lying – a dead cat . . .'

It is conceivable, then, she concludes this recollection, 'that it was some "dead cat" or other that was being burned'.[7]

What Erika did not know, and what would have frightened her even given her suspicions, was the entry her father made in his diary on 30 April, at the high point of his despair: 'My fears now bear first of all and almost exclusively on this assault on the secrets of my life. They are heavy and deep. Something frightful, even deadly, may happen.'[8]

This is a passage worth dwelling on rather longer than scholars have done up till now. The meaning seems clear, even if it may be construed in different ways. Does 'they' refer to the fears or to the secrets?[9] Thomas Mann's diaries are written in a style that presses ahead with its flow of thoughts, leaving fragments of sentences incomplete, so that 'they' are most likely the secrets; though the adjectives could apply to both, 'deep secret' is a well-established turn of phrase. Such heavy and deep secrets would also make sense of the 'fatal consequences', as only if they were heavy and deep could their disclosure have the most terrible effect.

But was it Mann himself whom these secrets indicated? In theory, his fears might have been for someone else, exposed in Germany to the vengeance of the Nazis and possibly in imminent danger by being named in this connection. This however is a far-fetched speculation and not the meaning immediately suggested, as is also confirmed from another source. Golo, in his auto-biography, quotes from the diary that he himself kept at this time. Thomas Mann had spoken about his fears in the family circle: 'They will publish excerpts in the *Völkischer Beobachter*. They will ruin everything, they will ruin me. My life will never be right again.'[10] The implication of suicide, if his secrets were exposed to the light of the world – that is strong stuff, even if we take into account that the nerves of the frightened man were extremely stretched at this time.[11] If the Nazis had concocted from these diaries a poisonous broth containing no more than those elements familiar from the surviving volumes, perhaps this alone would have been sufficient to make his life a torment? It would not have been found so natural in Munich that Thomas was in love with his own son;[12] his outbursts of hatred towards his brother would have been played upon, and the Nazis would have learned about the young Klaus Heuser, about the emotional adventure that gave rise to *Death in Venice*, and about the central experience of his early twenties, his youthful love for Paul Ehrenberg.[13] All this dished out to a scornful press free of any legal restraint – it is easy to imagine how such a campaign might destroy even a stronger person, so why not Thomas Mann, who took decades to digest lesser insults?

But so utterly shattered as to entertain thoughts of death? Even the new rulers of Germany would need something tangible, and they were still far from deciding how to deal with the Nobel prizewinner, a German national living legally abroad who at this point had still refrained from public declarations against the Nazi regime, and whose works were still available in the bookshops. There certainly was a group that sought in any event to get rid of him, but before his letter to the rector of Bonn University, there was still the vague possibility that he might return, and this tied the regime's hands. So the secrets really must have been heavy and deep, to give the enemy a deadly weapon that could strike its victim even on neutral territory.

Mann's recent commentators and biographers do indeed focus

on what they view as 'heavy and deep'. All of them, in so far as they have pondered the question, agree on one thing: the main secret, disclosure of which could have driven the author to suicide, was his 'inversion',[14] his love of boys, the homosexuality concealed behind the bourgeois façade – for which he supposedly felt a sense of guilt.[15] For a long while this key fact that stamps Mann's entire work was glossed over, as earlier biographers simply did not want to know too much. But since this prudery has evaporated, and the late diaries have come to light, the belief today is that a master key to his life and work has been discovered: it was boys, and this was likewise the issue in April 1933, when their admirer considered suicide.

At first sight this reading has everything in its favour. It seems to be confirmed by a further entry on that dramatic day when Thomas Mann thought of suicide. On arrival in Basle, unnerved and wracked with worry, he noted in the evening a touching detail: 'Katia and I sat holding hands a great deal. She more or less understands my fears concerning the contents of the suitcase.'[16] This is the one place however where a ray of light from outside strikes his inner thought process, the only moment at which we can emerge from his mind, tormented by worries, and see him through another's eyes. His wife Katia understands him 'more or less' – this may well refer to his young men, a subject on which she was more or less in the picture, even if they did not always bring it up at the breakfast table. Though this passage fits neatly into the traditional reading, it has a certain ambiguity. 'Of course I cannot tell her *everything*,' the young fiancé confided to his diary in 1904: 'She is not strong enough for my sorrow and torment.'[17]

How much did she know after thirty years of marriage? We know as little of this as of the way those secrets (in the plural) converge. One thing however we can say for certain: Katia was most likely aware very early on of her husband's erotic sufferings and tendencies, at the latest in 1927 after the Klaus Heuser affair. And so despite her 'more or less' understanding, there must still have been a part that was obscure.

A second detail that seems to support the conventional reading is quite similar. This is the word 'secret' itself, which in at least two places in the later diaries refers unambiguously to homosexuality. Five years before his death, Thomas Mann wrote about his last love, for the hotel page Franz Westermeier: 'Banal activity, aggressiveness, the attempt to discover how far he would go, is not part of my life, which requires a secrecy' (10 July 1950). And the 'compulsion to keep the secret' holds him back from seeking an encounter with Franz on the hotel terrace (11 July 1950). When he feared an assault on the secrets of his life, would this then have been one of them? That could be the conclusion drawn, were it not for this 'more or less'. One part lies open, but another remains concealed. There are indications where one secret certainly bears on the forbidden Eros, but this is interwoven with something worse.

IF YOU LIKE!

In the introduction he wrote in 1945 for an American edition of Dostoevsky's short novels, Thomas Mann held that the demonic should be addressed poetically: to devote critical essays to it struck him as indiscreet, to put it mildly. The present investigation could be reproached as highly indiscreet, since it pursues the question as to what hard evidence of homosexual contact might have been noted in the early diaries. This question, though, has been puzzled over since the later diaries were published, which Mann expressly entrusted to posterity with all the 'merry discoveries' that he dryly promised in this connection (13 October 1950). And it is precisely these later diaries that yield scattered indications as to the nub of the question, and allow us to correct the suppositions of recent biographers in two important respects.

We do not know for certain, writes the best of these, Hermann Kurzke, but it seems likely that in early life Mann had some kind of bodily contact that 'he experienced as demeaning, humiliating and besmirching, and that left a lifelong trauma. It might have been with young hustlers in Naples.'[18]

Kurzke is not the only biographer who brings on stage these Neapolitan hustlers, whom the young Thomas Mann may indeed have encountered; a scene that the traveller himself reveals when he writes to his close friend Otto Grautoff in 1896 that on the Toledo among a thousand other salesmen there are also procurers who in a sly hiss 'offer to escort you to supposedly "very pretty" young girls, and not only girls . . .'[19] Grautoff well understood what the ellipsis here was supposed to mean, all the more as the same letter contains a portrait of the city of Naples, 'a physiognomy with a rather snub nose and somewhat pouting lips, but very beautiful dark eyes . . .', which sounds more like that of a Neapolitan youth. To the complaint about the procurers, impossible to shake off, who extolled their wares to the point of coarseness, Mann adds the confession that he had almost decided on a rice diet, simply to rid himself of sexual desire.

Assuming for a start that he did not succeed in this, with or without the diet, and assuming further that at least once he did follow one of those hissing pimps – what is there to say against the idea that the young Thomas Mann could have had a homosexual encounter, and that as a world-famous author approaching sixty, he still found this experience so burdensome and compromising that he viewed its revelation as a deadly peril, as the ruin of his reputation, preferring rather to end his own life?

The evidence against this is the letters and diaries, a closer reading of which subtly shifts the perspective. For two things in particular emerge from these. First of all, that Thomas Mann quite clearly never went beyond a shy kiss with these youngsters. This is not to deny that his straying through the *mala vita* quarters of Naples and Rome is plausible; on the contrary. Simply that it can never have come to a fulfilled homosexual encounter. This was something denied him throughout his life, as all private indications suggest.

'Fulfilment,' though, is precisely the word he used, when less than a year after the suitcase episode he leafed through the rescued diaries and revisited his last passion: the friendship with Klaus Heuser, who had been a household guest in Munich in autumn 1927 and whom he had then visited several times in Düsseldorf. Mann was 'deeply roused, touched and moved' by looking back on this experience:

which seems to me today to belong to a different and stronger epoch of life, and which I retain with pride and gratitude, as it was the unhoped-for fulfilment of a lifelong yearning, the 'happiness' inscribed in the book of man, though not commonness, and remembrance of which signifies: 'I too'.

(24 January 1934)

This could still have all kinds of interpretation, and would raise the question what exactly he meant by 'fulfilment'. The same holds for another word that has a more explicit sound to less chaste ears:

Read for a long time old diaries from the Klaus Heuser time, when I was a happy lover. The most beautiful and touching occasion the farewell in Munich, when for the first time I took 'a leap into dreamland' and rested his temple on mine. Now indeed – lived and loved. Dark eyes that spilled tears for me, beloved lips that I kissed – this was it, I too had this, I can tell myself when I die.

(20 January 1942)

What Thomas Mann understood by being a lover emerges from an interview with Klaus Heuser at the age of seventy-seven. Nothing more took place than an embrace and a kiss, and the object of Mann's adoration could scarcely confirm even this; just the simple friendliness of a youngster who had in no way fallen in love, and realized almost nothing of the emotional magic he inspired.[20] For Thomas Mann, however, we know that this kiss was the high point of his erotic life. Klaus Heuser, indeed, so Mann wrote on 16 July 1950 in making a kind of balance-sheet of his amours, was the youth who 'permitted him most satisfaction'.

More vigorous homosexuals, however, aroused Mann's indignation. After reading Gore Vidal he noted: 'The sexual side, affairs with different men, I still find incomprehensible. How one can sleep with men' (24 November 1950). And even if boys rather than men are the issue, those who approach them bodily rouse his strong antipathy:

Finished the book on or against Gide's diary. Disgruntled against him by his all too direct sexually aggressive behaviour towards young people, without consideration or respect for them, without being ashamed of his age, soulless, really devoid of love. That I should expect something of this kind from a beloved youth! Unthinkable! To upset *his* admiration by vileness! Estrangement.

(6 October 1951)

But what if beside the beloved youths there were also unbeloved ones, if there were for Mann two strictly separate categories, one which embraced the divine boy who should not be too closely approached, and a second that comprised impersonal bodies and commercialized dolls of warm flesh? 'I would say, we should separate the sexual organs from love!' the twenty-year-old Mann instructed his friend Grautoff, simply following the bourgeois convention of his time.[21] This sounds rather like juvenile grandiloquence, and it also stands in sharp contrast with his own teaching, expressed in his work with almost religious verve, the postulate of a sacred love in which the most corporeal mingles and has to mingle with the most spiritual. Now this postulate might precisely serve as restitution and repentance for a heartless fall into adventures of the flesh. But there is a phrase which makes such completed adventures rather improbable. Half asleep, the old man dreams of taking leave of Franzl, the last of his beloveds and 'representative of the whole worshipped species', with a kiss. Indeed: 'Whether reality would *ever* have found me ready is a question in itself' (6 March 1951). No other meaning seems possible than that reality never put him to the test, beyond a mere kiss. Which leads us to conclude that in the early diaries, as far as the 'worshipped species' is concerned, the most that could be described is daydreams, in no way crude facts.

These daydreams, however, Thomas Mann had long made public. What supposedly appeared to him as an 'inexpressible danger', in case it was bruited about, he actually spoke about regularly for thirty years. Especially if we avoid the mistake of transposing the liberalism of today back to a time when it was very risky or even impossible to acknowledge oneself a homosexual, we might well admire the degree to which he ventured this. Thomas Mann wrote about homoeroticism with surprising openness and courage. 'The fact was that Tonio loved Hans Hansen, and had already suffered a good deal on his account,'[22] he wrote already in 1903 in *Tonio Kröger*, and the coming decades brought no alteration in this matter. Hans Castorp, too, loved Madame Chauchat only because her Kirghizian eyes made her appear to him as a re-embodiment of his youthful flame Hippe.

14

Neither Clavdia Chauchat nor Inge Holm nor any of the other dull female characters with whom Thomas Mann surrounds his heroes can stand up against the deeper attraction of a Hansen or Hippe.

Even if this could be read out of the picture, moreover, that would be hard to do with the tale of Gustav von Aschenbach. Here the final veil of camouflage falls away,[23] the female ancillaries are sent home, and the idolized Tadzio stands temptingly at centre stage. From 1912 at the latest, with *Death in Venice*, in which the protagonist who falls blindly in love with a boy is Mann's own thinly disguised alter ego, his open secret was known well outside the narrow circle around Stefan George. If twenty years later he was prepared to escape through death the disclosure of his homophilia, he would never have been able to publish the Venice story. Or he would have spent the time following its publication – under the Kaiser and before the freer era of the Weimar Republic – in a frightful state of agitation. Nothing would shield him from some reader or other being crude enough to say: 'Each word here comes from experience; there is nothing in it that was not coined exactly from his own life.'[24] Whatever the fears were that Thomas Mann had at this point – and of course he was nervous of criticism – they did not restrain him from developing over the years a concern of an exactly opposite kind. Had he slandered homoeroticism with the story of Aschenbach's demise? Carl Maria Weber made this kind of point to him, and he undertook energetic steps to rescue his reputation.[25] If only Herr Weber had been present at the discussion he had recently had one evening with Willy Seidel and Kurt Martens! It could not have escaped him then that *Death in Venice* was a celebration. And the author would certainly not want:

> you and others to have the impression that a mode of feeling which I respect because it is almost necessarily infused with *mind* (far more necessarily so, at any rate, than the 'normal' mode) should be something that I would want to deny or, insofar as it is accessible to me (and I may say that it is so in a scarcely qualified way), wish to disavow.[26]

That is excessively tortuous, no doubt – and in a fashion that we shall encounter again on another occasion – but it is unambiguous, and would be so even if he did not add in the same letter: 'Tell me whether one can "betray" oneself any better than that.'[27] He intended to betray himself, it was the addressee who was rather clumsy and slow on the uptake, so that three weeks later Mann had once again to add a final word:

> 'Scarcely qualified', in other words: almost unqualified. You did not understand this, and you praise me for my power of empathy. But that is not the way things are, and without a personal adventure the Goethe story would not have led on to Death i[n] V[enice].[28]

The false impression was thus erased, in the minds of Herr Weber and others. Thomas Mann did not deny that his feelings were those of Aschenbach; he denied that they were not. And if this denial was made to a small group – in which it would certainly circulate, and deliberately so – he was not shy before the wider public either. The letter to Weber was private, but that to Hermann Keyserling was public. Though its theme was 'On Marriage', Thomas Mann devoted long passages to homoeroticism and its double aspect of damnation and pride.[29] No one had raised this question with him. He spoke of it even when not asked, not just using an opportunity that arose, but seeking and forcing the opportunity even if it was not exactly suitable. 'I will venture in this connection, which remains a political one, and with all due caution and respect, to speak of the particular realm of feeling that was alluded to in my last remarks,' he declared in his speech on *The German Republic*, and we should be aware that he really was venturing somewhat, the 'nonpolitical' Thomas Mann of the *Reflections*, the adornment of reaction, standing before a conservative audience in Berlin's Beethovensaal in 1922 to declare that he had undergone a fundamental change and become a republican, and going on to justify this reversal, among other ways, by the fact that Walt Whitman in his phallically brimming fervour was the singer of democracy, and that democracy and male love stem from the same roots.[30] He was seeking to win over the *völkisch* youth who were terrorizing the republic in their secret male bands; this is the political context he refers to.[31] But the impression is given that there is scarcely a subject he speaks on that he would not bend in this sense to allow him a short visit to this region of feeling. When he wandered into it again personally, five years later at the time of Klaus Heuser, he never made any secret of this. 'No double life, it was something everyone knew.'[32]

So in 1933, then, was a mere kiss that had long been publicly fantasized enough to drive him to suicide? There is a distinction, of course, about whether what falls into the hands of the adversary are private records or literary works, just as there is a more forceful distinction between revealing oneself to a circle of accessories or being placed publicly in the pillory. But what kind of pillory would this have been? The darkness of those years should not prevent us from making minor distinctions. The raging persecution of homosexuals did not follow immediately on the Nazi seizure of power.[33] The sharpening of paragraph 175 came into force in September 1935; it was only from that point on that all sexual relations between men were penalized – as they were to remain until the end of Thomas Mann's life – as well as any intimate contact or kiss. The Röhm putsch, a decisive turning-point, was still a year away, and it is instructive how Mann commented on this. According to the customary reading, he found here a sharp and extreme version of the fate that might have threatened him, if his diaries had been rummaged. The murder of the homosexual Röhm and the campaign of the Nazi press – it was to be expected that he not only followed this news eagerly, but that his thoughts would wander back to April of the previous year, when he had feared he would himself become a victim of the new regime.

It was on 30 June 1934 that he learned of the 'mutiny of the SA and Röhm, who had been expelled and dropped by Hitler'. A short description of the events follows, with the usual disgust at the 'swamp of lies, crudeness and crime'. Two days later, on 2 July: 'The extent of stupid shamelessness is unimaginable, there has never been the like of it. Just as enormous is the silliness of making some kind of morality purge out of it, and speaking of a "cleansing storm".' 'Silliness,' that is his only word for it, which he had also used the previous day, in the only sentence he devotes to the supposed personal disgust that was the pretext given for the murder in Nazi propaganda: 'Hitler's operation against Röhm's villa in Wiessee, where Heines was surprised in bed with a young man and shot. A silly emphasis on the long acknowledged "moral failings".' That is all; he says nothing more on the subject. Is 'silly' the expression he would have used, if he saw here an example of something he had trembled over for a whole month? One would expect a stronger reaction, a glance back at the missing suitcase;[34] some word other than this tranquil expression, which is hard to reconcile with the previous year's hysteria.

But it fits exactly with something else. It fits with the tone in which Thomas Mann deals with his homoeroticism in all his remarks, a tone of surprising casualness and nonchalance. This is the second impression that emerges: Mann was never the type to see himself as a sinner on account of his sensual yearnings. Despite his Protestantism, he was never sufficiently 'Quakerish'[35] to feel guilt on account of his deviant desires. His work never displays any example of the kind of guilt feeling with which recent scholarship has sought to explain so much, a guilt that is supposed to thrive from an awareness of sexual deviation.[36] Why indeed should he feel guilty for something in which he was in the best artistic company, for something in which he also saw the foundation of his own artistic practice (6 August 1950) and which for all the problems it raised he accepted always as sacred – 'impossible here, absurd, depraved, ludicrous and sacred nevertheless', in his words about the declaration of love whispered by Aschenbach?[37] Sometimes we even seem to hear the very opposite. In the Franzl episode, he wrote in his diary that 'non-responsiveness' to the beauty of male youth was to him 'incomprehensible to the point of contempt' (28 August 1950). It is not remorse expressed here, much rather pride of belonging to an elite, however stigmatized. 'Platen and others, of whom I am not the lowest, have known this disheartening experience of shame and pain, which *however has its pride*' (11 July 1950). Shame and pride, but no sense of guilt. 'In fact,' he notes with this scarcely concealed pride in the essay on marriage, 'it is not good to denigrate or make fun of a zone of feeling that gave rise to the Medici memorial and David, the Venetian sonnets and the Pathétique in B-flat'.[38] It is one thing that sexuality was a cause of suffering for him throughout his life,[39] though even this had its occasional bright spots. But self-flagellation and a deadly taboo? The atmosphere of the diaries and letters is far removed from this. It is much freer than was long suspected in the case of the reserved Hanseatic burgher. One need only leaf a bit more through the entry that describes the suitcase episode. Scarcely a year later, he comments on Platen's ghazal, *I am as wife to man, as man to wife to you*: 'How his spiritual-ized passion, beyond eroticism, entered into my blood when I was in love!' (25 February 1934).[40] This is as little darkened by pangs of Protestant conscience as is his enthusiasm after seeing a German film when he reflects on the 'joy in youthful bodies', i.e. male bodies in their nakedness. This is a feature of German 'homosexuality' and is lacking among the attractions of French and American products: the depiction of young male nudity in flattering, even adoring, photographic illumination, whenever the occasion presents itself. [. . .] The Germans, or German Jews, who present this, are quite right: basically there is nothing 'more beautiful', and the idea that this 'most beautiful' is the most common of all, 'a daily occurrence' as I expressed it in 'Joseph', once again made me smile.

(4 February 1934)

If the cinema spectator seizes such an occasion to see homosexuality as a national characteristic, this indicates yet again how in no way did Mann feel personally condemned: the 'German' is as questionable and deep as he; no cause to feel himself chosen by Satan. Three months later he buried himself in his old notes from the time of his love for Paul Ehrenberg; the melancholy sense of that faded era spoke to him 'intimately and with deep sorrow', and in looking back he saw that he too had in his way experienced the all-too-human, had even been able to hold in his arms that which he yearned for. The experience with Klaus Heuser was 'a late surprise, with a quality of benign fulfilment about it but already lacking the youthful intensity of feeling, the wild surges of exultation and deep despair of that central emotional experience at twenty-five'.[41] The sentence with which he ends this retrospective should give cause for reflection to those interpreters who make such a great case out of the sense of deviation that allegedly consumed the paterfamilias in secret. Deviation is from a rule, a norm, a canon. What Thomas Mann understood by these things we can learn from the passage that immediately follows: 'This is doubtless the normal rule of human affections, and owing to this normality I can feel more strongly that my life conforms to the scheme of things than I do by virtue of marriage and children' (6 May 1934). This is more or less the opposite of what he should have said, if he had wanted to support the current received opinion.

Thomas Mann was no ascetic groaning under the scorpions of unwelcome desire. He was bold enough to have Goethe wake up in the seventh chapter of *Lotte in Weimar* with a morning erection. Behind the patrician façade of his household, things were different from how they were customarily imagined. No one took offence when Klaus brought back his various boyfriends, or Erika spent days in a drugged-out state. And for their part these two took no offence if their father asked them not to stand in the way of his latest conquest:

> I call him [Klaus Heuser] *du* and at our last farewell pressed him to my heart with his express consent. Eissi [Klaus] is requested to withdraw graciously and not disturb my circle. I am already old and famous, and why should it only be you who profit from this?[42]

Such was the tone in the Mann household. The late diaries show how the patriarch actually enjoyed it when the family teased him and made fun of his deep looks at waiters. When his heart was aching over Franzl, he noted: 'For the rest, nothing is dearer to me than if Erika jokes about these events, conversations with him, the present of five francs, etc.' (28 July 1950). Even in front of his wife, who found Franzl's eyes 'very flirtatious', he has no secrets here. 'I told her he had long been aware that I have a weakness for him' (12 July 1950). He turns round and round in his mind what exactly it is that enchants him about the divine youth. 'It must be lovely to sleep with him, but I don't have any special image of his limbs' (19 July 1950). Whatever it is that colours his passion, it is certainly no burning awareness of sin. Nor does he object to this passion being deduced from his work. 'Now, well and good,' he comments in his diary on Erika's remarks 'on the homosexual foundation of the novel' (3 March 1951). It is *Felix Krull* she refers to, returning to the subject again nine months later. 'Erika on the journey home on the arch-pederastic ("gay") character of the scene. Soit' (31 December 1951). The gesture of acceptance is always the same, also when his daughter tells him her suspicions about his favourite grandchild: 'Erika maintains over supper that Frido shows all the signs of homosexuality. I cast doubt on the possibility of drawing this conclusion from a childhood graceful-ness. [. . .] Anyway – so be it' (4 January 1949).

This acceptance is not something he displayed only within the family. With Adorno, too, he discussed the underlying homo-sexuality of *Doctor Faustus*.[43] And a year before his death he wrote to an acquaintance:

Your letter was [. . .] an interesting document, full of humour, and quite right in substance, even if a more widespread prac-tice of homosexuality (and it is indeed pretty widespread and

scarcely arouses offence) would scarcely be a sufficient meas-
ure against the stereotyping and dumbing-down of the world.
The inclination is not *that* widespread and will in all likelihood
never be so. As for me I am concerned, I am far from finding
fault if someone accuses me of it. If you like![44]

First, 'something frightful, even deadly may happen', and then
this 'if you like!' – the two hardly chime together. And if twenty
years lie between the two expressions, Mann's sovereign gesture
is not just the lassitude of old age. As early as 1920 little was lacking and he could have said the same 'if you like!'; with a certain
reservation he had already done so. In the letter to Weber mentioned above he confessed his emotional adventures before a
circle that he could not expect to remain silent on the subject;
indeed he expected just the opposite. This seems, to put it mildly,
not the most sensible way of keeping a secret whose disclosure
might leave only the option of suicide.

   Three days after he considered this worst of all steps, Thomas
Mann lay awake for a long while in the night, 'tormented by old
things'. These old things, which cannot be a permanent state as
his sexual inclination was, are mixed up in his thoughts with the
secrets: 'I could not sleep until 3 o'clock, tormented by old
things and especially by the affair of the suitcase, behind which
lurks a murderous peril' (2 May 1933). We do not know what
this suitcase concealed, but perhaps Mann's anxiety over the
secrets of his life was not just hysteria, perhaps these secrets
really were heavy and deep; perhaps across the decades the boy
question covered something that flared up for a moment that

black April, when he had reason to fear that the door of his innermost chamber would be broken open.

I HAVE WORSE THINGS TO FORGET

On the hundredth birthday of his father, Michael Mann presented his life's work in a major speech under the double star of *felix culpa*. What was happy or lucky in Thomas's life is easy to recognize, the 'basis of enjoyment and sunniness' that he still felt pervaded him in old age (27 August 1950). But the shadows that fell upon him could not be overlooked, and it was not only his son who traced the share of guilt.[45] Thomas Mann himself spoke of this guilt in defending himself against priestly attacks in the lecture 'My Time'. In post-war Germany, a religious board had denied his work any Christian character. Greater figures than himself had been attacked in this way, which awakened memories; in his own case however he had particular doubts, which related less to the content of his writings than to the impulse to which these owed their existence:

> If it is Christian to experience life, one's own life, as guilt, blame, duty, as the object of religious discontent, as something in urgent need of restitution, salvation and justification, then those theologians who maintain that I am characteristic of non-Christian writers are not quite correct. For in all likelihood it is seldom that the output of a life – even if this seems playful, sceptical, artistic and humorous – has arisen so completely,

from the beginning to its approaching end, from just this
frightening need for restitution, purification and justification,
as has my personal and so little exemplary attempt to practise
art.[46]

These are fine, even noble words, whose truth one need not
doubt, even if one can ask at the same time whether this is the
whole truth. Jacob Burckhardt confessed at the age of twenty that
he would at any moment exchange his life for never having been
born, and if it was possible, return into his mother's womb, even
though he had committed no crime and had grown up in favour-
able circumstances.[47] Thomas Mann's basic feeling seems to have
had a quite similar coloration, when he concluded his obituary on
his son Klaus with the words that one could hardly speak of
ingratitude for such an ambiguous and guilty present as that of
life.[48] For the disciple of Schopenhauer – or the born melancholic
– guilt lies not in what is committed or omitted, but rather in
being itself – a sexually aberrant being, in Mann's case, as the con-
sensus of recent research tends to believe.

One can only ask whether such a static guilt, the sin of a being
trapped by a blind will, explains the shadow over this particular
life, and whether it was sufficient stimulant for his work. Many
experts on Thomas Mann write as if they have doubts on this subject. In the words of Reinhard Baumgart, 'On a terrifyingly
narrow foundation of intensive experience and convulsion in life,
a veritable Gothic dome of structural richness will be erected.
Those who admire it may ask how this was possible; those whom
it dismays would like to know why it was so necessary.'[49] Hans

Wollschläger approaches the question with the same mixture of admiration and dismay, in his re-reading of *Doctor Faustus*:

> *Sense of sacrifice*, rather than sense of loss, is a sufficiently ambiguous designation for Mann's mood at work; what moves it is something especially active, and it was as deed, not as suffering, that Mann remained aware of it when he looked back with hindsight. Would this active force be the clue that leads to the *secret of his life?*[50]

Mann's lecture quoted above spoke not of deeds but of religious discontent, yet there are utterances of his in which guilt has a less passive stamp. In the 1909 essay 'Sleep, Sweet Sleep' he found words about sin which sound rather different from those of 'My Time':

> Only the Philistine considers that sin and morality are opposed ideas: they are one, for without knowledge of sin, without yielding to harm and destruction, all morality is nothing but sheer flabby virtuousness. It is not purity and innocence which are morally desirable, not cautious egoism and a contemptible knack at keeping a good conscience; not these, but the struggle and compulsion, the pain and passion, that make up morality.[51]

Philistine, flabby, egoism, contemptible – much is offered here to disparage the non-sinner and ennoble the bad conscience. The question arises – and it is always the same question – whether this disparaging is simply a disinterested consideration, or whether it is spoken *pro domo*, which seems indicated not just by the vigour of expression, but also by the autobiographical character of this very intimate text. At all events sin here is considered as something arising from struggle and compulsion, passion and pain, and not as something original that every human being has to bear.

Nor could the young Thomas Mann have had original sin in mind when he wrote to Grautoff from Rome of the 'Augean stable' of his conscience.[52] The following year he quoted from a poem of Platen, how 'The frightened heart has suffered / Desire and fear and dread', saying that this verse, in all its beauty, clarity and brevity, reflected his own condition with perfect accuracy.[53] Two years later, in winter 1900, he had 'really dreadful depressions with quite serious plans for self-elimination'. This was the onset of his love for Ehrenberg, with its torments and its 'indescribable, pure, and unexpected inner joy',[54] a time from which we have exultant letters of his as well as suicidal ones. It might seem for a moment that we had here 'the bad conscience, the sense of guilt, the anger at everything', which from his own youth he recognized in 'brother Hitler',[55] that what was responsible was simply youth with its idleness and the violent outbreak of indistinctly directed sexuality. But soon something quite different flickers into life again in the notes and letters. In January 1904 he replies to his brother Heinrich, who had reproached him for smuggling an attack on him into a review: 'You characterize it, in an extremely elegant paraphrase, as vile — well! I could defend myself [. . .]; but I don't want to forsake my deed, but instead accept responsibility for it — I have worse things to forget.'[56] But what exactly? Certainly not, it seems, the turmoil of sexuality, but deeds, actions, vileness and worse. Three years later the turmoil had for the time being ceased: he was married to a princess of a wife, in a state of unparalleled happiness, bathed in fame, his name pronounced only in hushed tones, he had two thriving children – making him 'a charlatan with a taste for excess and offensive in every sense'.[57]

What he describes with such irony in this autobiographical sketch – 'In the Mirror' – gives nothing away as to how he really feels inside. And it is easy to overlook the confession made in a letter to his publisher of the previous year, concealed as it is by the chatty tone. 'Work is difficult, and often enough a joyless and arduous nitpicking. But *not* to work – that is hell.'[58] Hell, we must conclude, is where he lives if he cannot reshape into his work the grief and torments of which he says nothing to Katia; and we remember here what he will later say about Dostoevsky: 'His life, which could not bear ultimate frankness, ultimate exposure before the eyes of the world, was ruled by the secret of hell.'[59]

The suffering does not vanish after *Tonio Kröger*, it undermines his middle years, and in old age assumes almost autocratic power. Since the publication of Mann's diaries, we know how serious he was in quoting Prospero's 'And my ending is despair'. His final years were racked by this despair. At the time of the Franzl turbulence in 1950, he wrote on 28 August: 'I still find *every* memory essentially painful, and orient myself completely to looking ahead'. The following year even this glance ahead becomes more sombre: 'I'm generally terrified of everything. My memories are

almost entirely painful, and the future seems to hold only renun-
ciation' (15 December 1951). From time to time there are still
'wayside images', glances at young men that give him a moment's
joy. But a further year later, in this deep, dark, final depression of
old age:

> My decline, my old age, shows itself in the way that love seems
> to have disappeared from me, and for a long while I have not
> seen a human face that I could mourn. My mood is now only
> lifted to kindness by the contemplation of animals – beautiful
> dogs, poodles and setters.
>
> (20 December 1952)

This should at least have eased his feelings of guilt, if the cause of
these was forbidden love. But their pressure did not decline; in
his final years Thomas Mann was concerned almost entirely with
forgiveness, the healing pendant of guilt. A long life accumulates
many reasons for feeling guilty, precisely in the case of the self-
seeking artist, who scrounges off life as the 'vampire' of art does
on him,[60] and in whose shadow so much withers.[61] It can certainly not have been this artist's sense of guilt, nor even the
semi-religious Schopenhauerian version – however strongly they
may both form undercurrents or superstructures on a more specific guilt feeling – that connects with the 'old things' set down in
black and white in the early diaries, in such terms that their
exploitation by the enemy would have been enough to drive him
to suicide. And it is neither original sin nor the guilt of the egocentric artist that in his late work calls for forgiveness, the idea

around which the late work circles. The primary guilt there is action, not being.

This is also how Thomas Mann viewed the writer who he believed to inhabit hell. In Dostoevsky there could be no mis-understanding as to what particular sense of guilt his life's work was based on. In his 1945 essay, Mann expressed himself in words quite similar to those he was to use five years later in 'My Time'. But now with a significant addition:

> Undoubtedly the subconscious and even the consciousness of this titanic creator was permanently burdened with a heavy sense of guilt, a sense of the criminal – and this feeling was by no means of a purely hypochondriac nature.[62]

At the root of Dostoevsky's sense of guilt, therefore, Thomas Mann finds not the God-seeking Russian soul – which would have made it so easy to reinterpret this guilt feeling in a metaphysical sense – but rather something tangible, something 'non-hypochondriac'. If we bear in mind the supreme, indeed sacred place that the Russian writer assumed in his life, likewise that this introduction was contemporary with the writing of *Doctor Faustus*; if we recall that this novel almost obtrusively puts Dostoevsky alongside Nietzsche and that the portrait of Leverkühn is by his own confession a self-portrait; if we then bring in the fear over the deadly secrets of the diaries, then a certain suspicion begins to arise. It is the inkling that on this occasion, too, Mann did the same as he had done in his portraits of Chamisso, Kleist and Platen, of Goethe, Schopenhauer, Gide, Verlaine, of Wagner,

Michelangelo, Chekhov and Schiller: 'In my productions I reveal myself with such passion that a few indiscretions against others scarcely come into consideration.'[63]

This is what Thomas Mann wrote in 1904, and he remained faithful to this confession also in his essays. All critical writings, whatever they may reveal about their subject, are for him simply opportunities for that passion, only expressions 'with you as their occasion', as he put it in his early apologetic *Bilse und ich*; and as applies to them all: 'It is not you I discuss, on no occasion, please be consoled, but me, myself . . .'[64] This holds at least for the above-named series whose self-revealing character is so well known and attested by scholarship that it borders already on the trivial. It is only in the case of Dostoevsky that no one as yet has turned the view of the subject portrayed back to the portrayer himself. We may hesitate somewhat in making this move, but the question can still not be avoided whether at the end of the day, the guilt feeling of this gigantic creator was likewise of a non-hypochondriac kind.

With this question, or inkling, the point is reached at which one might well falter: would it not be better to break off the discussion and withdraw to the safer terrain of *ignoramus, ignorabimus*? But it is Mann himself who signals us on. By the detour of illness, which is 'clearly and unambiguously sexual in origin', he traces Dostoevsky's guilt to a traumatic event and an early crime. In *Crime and Punishment* it is said of Svidrigailov that his past concealed a 'criminal case with a flavour of bestial and as it were fantastical crudeness, for which he would in all likelihood have been sent to Siberia'. As Thomas Mann explains:

It is left to the more or less willing imagination of the reader to guess what this affair might be: in all probability it is a sex crime, possibly a child rape – for this is also the secret or a part of the secret in the life of Stavrogin in *The Possessed*, that icy and contemptible masterful person before whom weaker creatures grovelled in the dust, possibly one of the most weirdly attractive characters in world literature.

In one section of the novel, Stavrogin confesses an assault on a young girl, a violent fragment 'full of a terrible realism transcending the bounds of art' (almost literally the same description that he was to give shortly after of his own *Doctor Faustus*).[65] Precisely this, the violation of a child, was – as Thomas Mann only indicates in the preface, but in an early letter treats as a credible *on dit* – the crime that sunk Dostoevsky's life into a sense of heavy guilt.[66]

The subject here, however, was not Fyodor Dostoevsky, but sinister characters in world literature. Without troubling himself overmuch, Mann bridges here a gulf that is theoretically forbidden. The author in flesh and blood is one thing, the character made of ink something else, and any conclusion drawn from the latter to the former inevitably courts the reproach of mingling or confusing the two spheres. It is a reproach which Mann himself would have heard, in common with many other readers, had it already been raised at a time when the insulting term 'biographism' had not yet been coined. He read Dostoevsky as Freud and Proust had read him,[67] and drew from the inner life of his characters conclusions about the life of their creator, thus basing a biographical assumption on fiction. Whether or not this is permissible is an academic question, which cannot be avoided,[68] but which need not however divert us from the obvious. And what is obvious is that the gulf between life and fiction was indeed bridged by the author, that this was his habit, that he could not do otherwise, and that this appeared self-evident to him. This is how he reads; this is how he can be read. Before we retreat therefore to the safe ground of the unknowable, let us follow his invitation to do what immediately suggests itself. We get no confession in the style of Stavrogin; his 'idea of a gruesomely monotonous confession of guilt in the Russian style,' as Mann put it in 1951, he had never carried out.[69] But he does not tire of repeating that his writing is strongly auto-biographical, that he always speaks only of himself, and that he can say, even has to say, that he had '*never* invented anything'.[70]

The early diaries were burned. Thomas Mann took his secrets with him into his tomb. But this was a tomb in the Egyptian style: the palatial edifice of his work.

CHAPTER TWO

'VOLUPTUOUSNESS AND HOT GUILT'

I N 1935, WHEN Thomas Mann was poised to depict the fate of the lovesick Mut-em-inet, the chaste wife of Potiphar who fell for the young steward Joseph, he interpolated a private reflection on the unity of his work. This was, he wrote with evident emotion, always the same:

> it is the idea of a catastrophe, the invasion of destructive and wanton forces into an ordered scheme and a life bent upon self-control and a happiness conditioned by it. The saga of peace wrung from conflict and seemingly assured; of life laughingly sweeping away the structure of art; of mastery and overpowering, and the coming of the stranger god — all that was there from the beginning, as it was in the middle. And in a late age which is aware of its affinity with human beings, we find ourselves still united with them in that bond of sympathy.[1]

The 'middle' here refers to *Death in Venice*, where the artistry of Gustav von Aschenbach was shattered. The 'beginning' would be the story *Little Herr Friedemann*. In a letter that is often quoted, but seldom taken quite seriously, Thomas Mann said of this work, dating from 1896, that up till then he still needed a secret diary, but from then on he found for the first time the 'discreet forms and masks' under which he could parade his experiences among the public.[2] The remark is striking, and far more so than has ever been realized; not only because it knows no gulf between truth and fiction and the story now replaces the diary, not only because he situates his future work completely under the sign of masquerade and camouflage,[3] but also because he speaks of experiences, not of dreams, imaginings or fantasies.

Johannes Friedemann – like Dunja Stegemann or Paolo Hofmann one of the ego-substitutes that bear their autobiographical stamp in their very name[4] – the little Herr Friedemann, marked by a bodily defect, oriented himself early in life towards a dry, well-ordered contentment without the fulfilment of love, until he came under the spell of Gerda von Rinnlingen. This masculine Gerda, smoking and swinging her whip, he finds irresistibly attractive. When she inquires about his stigma he stammers out a confession, and when she subsequently rejects him, he drowns himself in the river. It seems hard to imagine a more innocent and defenceless victim, and this is precisely how the narrator of *Joseph and His Brothers* presents it when he looks back at these dramas of affliction, in the first of which the poor Herr Friedemann is swept away by cruel life.

If we examine the story more closely, however, we find that there is something else going on as well. Friedemann's erotic humiliation acts on him as an ever more strongly rising emotion. When Gerda shames him for the first time with her glances, the pale man grows still paler, and 'a strange, bitter-sweet rage welled up inside him'. This anger grows into an 'impotent, voluptuous hatred', shoots through him as an 'impotent; sweet, agonizing fury', and it is also this insistently depicted, pleasurable rage that drives him to self-destruction.[5] When Gerda laughingly flings him to the ground and he lies in the water, he asks himself what exactly is going on in his mind:

> Perhaps it was that same voluptuous hatred he had felt when she humbled him with her eyes; and now that he was lying here on the ground like a dog she had kicked, did this hatred per-haps degenerate into an insane fury which had to be translated into action, even if it was only action against himself?[6]

Voluptuousness and insane fury – that is rather different from the sound of shawm or cor anglais that has been heard for so long in Mann's work, the *Tristan* theme of love and death. For close to a century, the eroticism and metaphysic of death covered up what was rumbling below the surface of this work. Underneath it was not the entrancement of love and death, but rather the pangs of desire and violence.

Little Herr Friedemann still directs this violence against him-self. His tale stands at the beginning of a series of fictions, which all revolve around the same motif. *The Joker*, *Tobias Mindernickel*, *The Wardrobe*, *Revenge*, *Little Lucy* and *The Road to the Churchyard* all deal with outsiders, with deep humiliation and uncontrollable rage.[7] From 1897, however, after Thomas Mann's second journey to Naples, a certain change occurs: the rage of the humiliated party is discharged as aggression. The story that dates from the Roman summer of 1897 treats of a timid recluse, in whom – the words of an early review – 'goodheartedness and human bestiality sleep closely together'.[8] Tobias Mindernickel is his name, a man whom children shout funny rhymes about on the street, and who only gets into a gentle mood if he can commiserate with the sorrows of others. One day Mindernickel goes for a walk over the Lerchenberg, where a salesman has a young hunting dog on a lead. Tobias circles him three times, asks the price with downcast eyes and in low, hurried tones – a scene distantly related to the sale of the shadow in *Peter Schlemihl*[9] – and takes his new companion home, giving him the name of Esau.[10] When Esau gets boisterous, Mindernickel is seized like Herr Friedemann by a 'mad and extravagant fit of anger', and he beats the disobedient dog. After this chastisement he poses in front of the dog like Napoleon before a defeated regiment,[11] Mann's hero of this era, whose portrait stood on his writing desk. When Esau has the misfortune to injure himself on a kitchen knife, his master cares for him devotedly. Once the animal is well again, however, his mood reverses. 'His face was drawn with suffering, and he followed Esau's pranks unmoving, with a sidelong, jealous, wicked look.'[12] Mindernickel was pale like Friedemann, pale like the criminal face in Dostoevsky,[13] pale like many later characters of Mann's. The train of events that follows is described by the narrator as 'sinister, to an extraordinary degree':[14]

That which now happened was so shocking, so inconceivable, that I simply cannot tell it in any detail. Tobias Mindernickel stood leaning a little forward, his arms hanging down; his lips were compressed and the balls of his eyes vibrated uncannily in their sockets. Suddenly with a sort of frantic leap, he seized the animal, a large bright object gleamed in his hand – and then he flung Esau to the ground with a cut which ran from the right shoulder deep into the chest. The dog made no sound, he simply fell on his side, bleeding and quivering . . .[15]

The insane rage is no longer directed self-destructively against the hero, but against the hated and loved dog which Tobias Minder-nickel murders. This is not the last dog in Mann's opus with a violent end in store, nor the last knife that we see shining there. And Tobias Mindernickel, as has been noted, bears the initials of his creator.

On his return to Munich, Thomas Mann completed the following year a further 'story full of riddles' as its subtitle puts it, The Wardrobe, of which he occasionally said that quite against his custom he had written it 'under the influence of a hot toddy' and the signs of this could be seen.[16] This tells of the mortally ill Albrecht van der Qualen, who breaks off his train journey to Rome and alights at a town modelled on Lübeck, where he lodges at a small boarding-house – that is, unless he has in fact dozed off on the train and simply dreamed the whole thing. In his room, which also contains Mann's massive mahogany bed, is a ward-robe, and in the evenings a naked girl appears in it and tells him stories. The only one of these stories that the reader gets to hear has a disturbing conclusion:

But it ended badly; a sad ending: the two holding each other indissolubly embraced, and while their lips rest on each other, one stabbing the other above the waist with a broad knife – and not without good reason. So it ended.[17]

Rage against the humiliation suffered is laconically transformed here into the 'good reason' for which one party is stabbed to death. The careful avoidance of a gendered pronoun is striking. Mann resorts to this uncommon usage in order, presumably, not to say explicitly that the couple is homosexual, otherwise there would be no reason not to make the genders clear and circumvent so awkwardly the question whether it is the man who sticks the knife into the woman, or vice versa.

Just as striking are the distorting prisms that Thomas Mann interposes before the brute fact. The event 'A stabs B' is not related by a narrator as something experienced or faithfully recounted, it is placed in a fairy-tale, and this tale is not related by a real character, but by an unreal dream figure, whose hearer in all likelihood is also dreaming, asleep on the express train to Rome.

The motive – which by this device is shifted into the furthest realm of unreality – occupies Mann also in projects of which we have only indirect knowledge. Peter de Mendelssohn, his first biographer, writes in his commentary on this fairy-tale's irritating conclusion:

'Above the waist', it is expressly said, not below. Murderers impelled by robbery, by lust, or just plain murderers, re-occur with their knives quite frequently in the imaginings of the young writer – not least in the aforementioned plans for stories not completed, from 'Murderer Schandfleck' to 'Murderer Ocean'. They must indeed have had 'good reason'.[18]

A knife even turns up in *Buddenbrooks*, where it is not so easily smuggled in. The miraculous work of the twenty-five-year-old writer, the great bourgeois family novel, leaves little room for the kind of scandalous happenings depicted in *Tobias Mindernickel* or *The Wardrobe*; outward appearances are important in Mengstrasse, where knives should be raised only at dinner. But there is a member of this senatorial family who does occasionally lose his composure. This is Christian, the outsider and failure, to whom Thomas Mann ascribed all those portions of himself that he could not safely deposit on Hanno or his namesake Thomas. Thomas Buddenbrook upholds the achievement ethos, he is the fragile hero of the will; Hanno is the sensitive latecomer, while it is Christian who receives all the odd and neurasthenic qualities that his master surreptitiously endows him with. Not only does he share the insecurity, the tendency to buffoonery, escapism and decadence which Thomas Mann had to combat in himself.[19] He also tells strange stories, which he draws from the experience of his author.

We don't know whether Mann actually believed that all the nerves of his left side were too short. But we do know that something far more improbable which he has the sick Christian come out with, is taken from autobiographical fact. 'Perhaps it happens to you,' Christian asks when aroused to struggle against his brother, 'that you come into your room when it is getting dark and see a man sitting on your sofa, nodding at you, when there is no man there?'[20] He refrains from saying that this man was the Devil, but otherwise this is just the experience that the prospective author of *Buddenbrooks* had in Palestrina, and is conjured up once again in chapter 25 of *Doctor Faustus*.[21] Now if even this most mythical of experiences has a kernel of fact, and if Christian himself in this apparent nonsense says nothing but the truth, then caution is indicated about lesser stupidities; they may well be true. This must at all events be borne in mind with the other cock-and-bull stories he tells to amuse his family:

> But Christian did not hear. His eyes roamed about, sunk in thought, and he soon began to tell a story of Valparaiso, a tale of assault and murder of which he had personal knowledge . . . 'Then the fellow ripped out his knife – '[22]

This is the first time that the word murder has been dropped, since Tony so stubbornly and unbelievably confused the first name of her Morten Schwarzkopf with the word *'Mord'*.[23] Thomas is unwilling to hear all this, and gives the impression 'that he thought Christian was exaggerating and joking . . . which was certainly not the case'. Differently now from *The Wardrobe*, where he could not draw unrealistically enough away, this time the narrator decently insists that everything really did take place as he described. No exaggeration and no jest: Christian had been present in person at the scene of a murder at which knives were drawn, in the south, one may suppose in the criminal underworld in which the romancer was at home, as is mentioned two pages

later. We are in no way told, however, that he felt guilty for wit-
nessing this event; Protestantism and conscience in this novel are
ascribed to the Schopenhauer reader Thomas.

The two things are combined, however, the decadent and the
moralist, in the protagonist of the short story that appeared in
1903, and to which, right into his old age, Thomas Mann remained particularly tied. Tonio Kröger, the young artist, who
from the depths of his being loves the allure of the surface, has
much in common with both Hanno and Thomas, and no less so
with the impressionable Christian. He too comes into contact
with knives, even if this time they are not drawn as weapons. In
Tonio Kröger, the knives appear only in a blunted form, trans-
figured by literature: in the 'sword-dance of art',[24] the dance of
Andersen's little mermaid, which forty years later becomes a
major theme in *Doctor Faustus*.[25] It is a new technique that Mann
embarks on here, a new way of telling the old business. The cruelty is no longer shifted into a dreamscape as in *The Wardrobe*,
neither is it placed at a curious margin as in *Buddenbrooks*; this
time it is given pompous significance and symbolically enhanced.
All three techniques that Mann felt his way towards and expanded
with ever greater virtuosity belong from now on to his secure
stock-in-trade; they no longer change till the very end, and are
resurrected from one work to the next.

The enhancing idealization, which is shown from *Tonio Kröger*
onwards, does not prevent this tale from being so bluntly autobiographical that its author even signed letters 'Tonio Kröger'.[26]
There are not many details in the story which we could not
say where they fit in real life. Even the episode from the travel

chapter is taken from Mann's own experience, when at an hotel in his home town Tonio Kröger is questioned by the police, who confuse him with a man they are pursuing 'for various frauds and other offences'. After the misunderstanding is cleared up, the hotelier apologizes to the unjustly accused hero:

> 'The officer was of course only doing his duty, though I told him at once that he was on the wrong track . . .'
> 'Really?' thought Tonio Kröger.[27]

An extremely sybilline thought, reminiscent of the very suggestive silence that Kröger maintains in response to a question from Lisaveta, the painter friend in whose studio he delivers his monologues on art. He tells her about a banker who in his free time has written short stories, despite – 'I call it "despite"' – not exactly being innocent enough for this sublime vocation. On the contrary, he has already served a prison sentence, 'and for good reason', as Kröger almost literally quotes from *The Wardrobe*. It was in prison, in fact, that the banker first became aware of his talent, which leads Tonio Kröger to conclude that 'it is necessary to have been in some kind of house of correction if one is to become a writer'. Lisaveta asks him whether it is only other artists he has in mind. But Tonio Kröger doesn't answer: 'He did not reply. He contracted his slanting brows in a frown and whistled to himself.'[28]

This silence and whistling says enough – put into words, Kröger himself is no stranger to the experiences, or should one say actions, that were good reason for his criminal colleague to be sent to prison. But what could those experiences have been? There is only one earlier passage that gives us some indication of this. In the third chapter we learn something about the recent past of the runaway bourgeois scion:

> He lived in large cities in the south, for he felt that his art would ripen more lushly in the southern sun; and perhaps it was heredity on his mother's side that drew him there.[29] But because his heart was dead and had no love in it, he fell into carnal adventures, far into voluptuousness and hot guilt, although such experiences cost him intense suffering.[30]

In the south he fell into carnal adventures, the man who signed himself Tonio Kröger; this has already been assumed by his recent biographers. But the burning guilt that he speaks of here is something that scholarship has yet to track down.

It is certainly guilt of a non-hypochondriac kind, a misdeed in the same region where Dostoevsky found his own descent into hell. This could all be taken as empty boasting, to bring some blood into the veins of the pallid hero.[31] But it doesn't end with Tonio Kröger, any more than it began with him, and everything that follows is coloured by the same voluptuousness and hot guilt.

'I KNOW WHAT BLOOD IS'

Dripping, running, flowing blood – over time Thomas Mann depicts even its physical trace ever more accurately. The flow of blood is present even in what would seem to be quite innocent asides. One of these is the innocuous tale that he wrote a year before the less innocuous *Death in Venice*, and which tells nothing more or less than its title promises: *The Fight Between Jappe and Do Escobar*. This records a memory from a holiday experience in Travemünde, an impending scrap between two adolescents, which was announced to the narrator, a boy of thirteen, by his friend Johnny Bishop. This Johnny, lying naked on his back next to him, is a 'thin little Cupid', his manner 'a little like a woman who preserves her youth'; with his mocking smile and girlish eyes he ensures that the theme of sexual confusion is present even on holiday.[32] Jappe and Do Escobar, admired ruffians who in the evenings shared the amusements of the grown-ups, were at loggerheads over a 'gal', and hold their duel in public on the beach. Onlookers gather, the fight begins, and comes to an end without too much damage. Only a blow to Do Escobar's nose leaves the trace to which Thomas Mann is irresistibly drawn: 'The blood ran between his fingers onto his clothes, it soiled his light trousers and dropped down on his yellow shoes.'[33] Despite the nosebleed the scrap was harmless, but in the imagination of the narrator, who feverishly awaits it, it takes threatening forms. He dreads the shock that the sight of a bitter struggle would arouse in him, a 'duel *à outrance*', a 'fight for life and death'; in a day-dream he feels with the fighters, senses their 'flaring, shattering hatred, the attacks of raving impatience' and revenge, and strikes out 'blind and bloody with an adversary just as inhuman'.[34] Life-and-death struggle as a kind of introspective shadow-play: a new and elegant way of bringing something distant close, or pushing something close away.

A second theme is also developed in the works of this period, and over the decades grows steadily more important. A bloody deed is not only mentioned by the narrator, the culprit himself has to come out with it at some point. Tonio Kröger knew how to speak through silence, but this silence is no longer enough, and the need for confession, for an unburdening admission, grows ever more compelling. In *The Magic Mountain*, in the *Joseph* novels, *Doctor Faustus* and *The Holy Sinner*, it is vented in long prepared scenes of confession.

The liberating outburst of admission arises already in the *Anecdote* of 1908, in connection with the theme of a double life.[35] At the end of a festive supper, the host Herr Becker, husband of the universally beloved young Angela, is assured once again how much he is envied, congratulated and blessed on account of his wife. 'Suddenly all went quiet, as Becker stood up, Director Becker, pale as death. For once – the words were wrestled from his breast – for once he had to say it! For once unburden himself of the truth, which he had borne for so long alone!' And the paralysed, dumbstruck guests who witness this mad outbreak, some sitting, some standing up – the scene anticipates Leverkühn's final confession in *Doctor Faustus* – scarcely believe their ears when Becker draws a picture of his marriage, 'his *hell* of a marriage'.[36] The angelic Angela is in truth a monster, false, mendacious, and horrific. Becker blurts out:

How the whole day long her only activity is to find new and ghastly ways of torturing her cat. How she torments him mercilessly with her spiteful moods. How she shamelessly betrays him, and cuckolds him with servants, with tradesmen, even with beggars who come to the door.

Not a dog this time, but a cat; yet once again, torment is paired with lust. Unlike on later occasions, however, here it is not his own guilt that the sinner confesses after a long time of silence. This confession is an accusation, but the guilt affects the accuser too: the pale man cries to the assembled company how Angela has also drawn him 'into the whirlpool of her depravity, how she has humiliated, stained and poisoned him'.[37]

What precisely this means remains uncertain; but 'poisoned' anticipates once again a theme in *Faustus*, in which Leverkühn accuses himself of a poisonous influence on his beloved boy. The Devil, one of whose names is the 'poison angel', the false Angela, has seduced them both, and pulls them both down into the jaws of hell. Both of them are sent to a mental home after their confessions.

The confidence trickster Felix Krull comes to a similar end. This novel, a fragment of which Mann had already started to write in 1910, and which promises its confessions in its very title, does not seem to show the slightest sign of hellish guilt. The Sunday child Felix sins without any pangs of conscience, and falls with the greatest pleasure into the abyss into which the bad love teacher Rosza entices him.[38] With her, the Hungarian whore with the boyish body and the almost grim seriousness that will re-appear in both *Joseph* and *Faustus*, Felix learns all about sensuality and doesn't even think of feeling guilty on this account. The only thing reminiscent of Dostoevsky is his epilepsy, and even this is just something he fakes for his doctor. At the very margin, however, violence lurks even in this case. It threatens him from the masters of these 'birds of death', the pimps. Felix Krull fears their knives, 'with which they make so free'.[39] He himself becomes Rosza's pimp, even if he rejects this ugly word. His predecessor, a former butcher's apprentice, has been imprisoned 'on account of some bloody deed'.[40]

And at the end, for all his jolly adventures, Felix too would have rotted in prison, just like Tonio Kröger's criminal banker. It is easy to forget that Krull writes his memoirs in jail. A passage in Thomas Mann's diaries indicates that he may have landed there for more serious reasons than confidence trickery: 'K[atia] told me of the murder of a postman delivering money orders by a gentleman criminal at the Hotel Adlon. Noted this for my arrangements for the confidence trickster' (5 January 1919). We do not know whether the trickster himself was to repeat these arrangements, whether he was to be a witness, an accomplice, a foil; but that some bloody deed had to make its appearance even in this burlesque story of the child of fortune says something about the urgency of a theme with which Thomas Mann was himself 'so free'.

What had enchanted him about *Felix Krull* was the 'directness of the autobiographical form', as he writes in *A Sketch of My Life*.[41] But he gets far more direct in his next work, again narrated in the third person.

The 'wanderer' at the Northern Cemetery, the dreary Pula boat, the grey-haired rake, the sinister gondolier; Tadzio and his family, the journey interrupted by a mistake about the luggage, the cholera, the upright clerk in the Travel Bureau, the rascally ballad-singer, all that and anything else you like.'[42]

Everything in *Death in Venice* was drawn from reality, just as in *Tonio Kröger*, to which Mann expressly refers. Thus the last in this series is also drawn from life, and we have even less reason to doubt the ballad-singer's reality, in so far as he seems strangely familiar even to those of us left at home. His decisive appearance he spares himself until *Faustus*. But as early as 1903 he strolls through the study *The Hungry*. In this, a writer named Detlef has a shocking nocturnal encounter after a visit to the theatre. It is two o'clock in the morning, snow is falling, and carriages are waiting, just as in Krull's first encounter with Rosza, when Detlef sees a distressing sight: a man in ragged clothing stares at him, a savage, hollow face with a red beard and an expression of vile contempt; and this lecherous and greedy examination is something that he 'could never get over, could not put out of his mind. . .'[43] This man seems the same type as the minstrel from *Death in Venice*, who with an 'insolent bravado', no beard but still red-headed, 'thin and cadaverous in the face', has a way of 'lasciviously licking the corner of his mouth' and directs his scornful laughter up to the terrace where Aschenbach is gripped in a posture of defence or flight.[44] He will work his way up to the Devil before whom Leverkühn falls in a frozen rigidity. But already in *Death in Venice* we learn what his particular character is: 'He was quite evidently not of Venetian origin, but rather of the race of Neapolitan comedians, half pimp, half actor.'[45]

How is Aschenbach so familiar with the race of Neapolitan pimps? Naples seems gradually to emerge from behind Venice, as it were, as soon as the bewitched Aschenbach loses his self-control. Vicious riff-raff start to make the streets unsafe at night, muggings and even murders become common, and 'commercial vice [takes] obtrusive and extravagant forms, hitherto unknown in this area and indigenous only to southern Italy or oriental countries'.[46] It is the south again where Tonio Kröger goes astray, not without moments of awareness and shame. '"How far astray I have gone!" he would sometimes think,'[47] and Aschenbach thinks the same when he follows the boy through dirty alleys: 'Where is this leading me! he would reflect in consternation.'[48]

What precisely these paths were, Thomas Mann lets slip again a while later, in a little-noticed passage. In 1928 he published an enthusiastic article on Bruno Frank's *Politische Novelle*, which in its tone and many details is obviously modelled on the tale of Aschenbach's demise. The grateful teacher gives a review that reads like a monologue on *Death in Venice*. Bruno Frank's setting is Marseille, but it could also be Venice, 'stylized completely in the demonic and ghostly fashion, to the point of nightmare, frightening, dangerously seductive, the well-behaved soul completely estranged, immoral entrancement through and through'. In this story the hero gets lost in a red-light district and finds himself exposed to 'the horrific primeval assault of a street of brothels'. This really must be called unsurpassable, writes the visibly moved reviewer,

the loss of one's way in those blind alleys and traps, where the man who has consciously and deliberately forsaken the 'path of reason' stumbles upon the dark and deadly sweet image of a woman from a distant land, who awakens his blood to a destructive love.

This is full of echoes and resonance; so too is the phrase that sums up the action of the concluding chapter, and has to be deciphered in the same way as the tortuous confession in the letter to Weber about the type of feeling that is accessible to Mann 'in a scarcely qualified way'. Carmer, the tragic hero of Bruno Frank's tale, 'is absorbed by the *mala vita* quarter of the evil city and falls into a decline, in a manner that is mysterious, yet not undecipherable in terms of a feeling close to his way of being'.[49] What does this tortuous sentence mean? Whose feeling recognizes a similar being here? The '*mala vita* quarter', one should note in passing, is not a French but an Italian expression for the red-light district of Marseille. It is not a term used in Bruno Frank's story.[50]

Carmer is finally stabbed to death in the arms of the prostitute. Aschenbach dies a gentler death from cholera. The outbreak of the epidemic also gives Thomas Mann the opportunity to speak of the second part of Tonio Kröger's experience. For Aschenbach, too, the south holds an intimate combination of sensuality and guilt. This guilt lies not in the fact that it is a boy whom Aschenbach desires, but rather in the fact that he risks the boy's life. Aschenbach is an accessory who remains silent and fails to prevent harm, even relishing this: 'The consciousness of his complicity in the secret, of his share in the guilt, intoxicated him, as small quantities of wine intoxicate a weary brain.'[51]

The narrator explains in the same chapter why Aschenbach

does not warn Tadzio's family of the cholera: 'to passion, as to crime, the assured everyday order and stability of things is not opportune,' and so it must welcome 'any chaos and disaster'.[52] A comparison, no more, in which passion goes hand-in-hand with crime. But there are other ways of speaking of crime, as the early work shows: concealment at a curious margin, symbolic enhancement, and removal into dream. The two last means are combined extremely effectively in *Death in Venice*. The turning-point in Aschenbach's passion is a fearful dream; only after this is he ready for his decline. What does he dream about? The stranger-god Dionysus, who descends on the valley with his maenads and carries on orgies, as Nietzsche's friend Rohde has depicted in *Psyche*. Not reality, a dream, and not a personal dream, but a symbolic scene from mythology and the history of ideas. The double transfer has been quite effective, in that external sources are still sought for Aschenbach's nightmare, and the trail of blood that leads to Mann's early work is overlooked.

At first Aschenbach defends himself. 'Great was his loathing, great his fear, honourable his effort of will to defend to the last what was his and protect it against the Stranger, against the enemy of the composed and dignified intellect.'[53] But then Aschenbach's resistance breaks: 'His heart throbbed to the drumbeats, his brain whirled, a fury seized him' – the old fury of Herr Friedemann –,

a blindness, a dizzying lust, and his soul craved to join the round-dance of the god. The obscene symbol, wooden and gigantic, was uncovered and raised aloft: and still more unbridled grew the howling of the rallying-cry. With foaming mouths they raged, they roused each other with lewd gestures and licentious hands, laughing and moaning they thrust the prods into each other's flesh and licked the blood from each other's limbs.[54]

Here, mythologically enhanced and graphically illustrated, is the old recipe from *Tonio Kröger*, sensuality and blood, pupated into dream. And Aschenbach wades deeply in:

But the dreamer now was with them, and in them, he belonged to the stranger-god. Yes, they were himself as they flung themselves, tearing and slaying, on the animals and devoured steaming gobbets of flesh, they were himself as an orgy of limitless coupling, in homage to the god, began on the trampled, mossy ground.[55]

The theme has come a long way from the days of Tobias Mindernickel who stabbed his dog, from the days of *The Wardrobe* with its murderous embrace. But at its core nothing has changed.

One thing, however, is now added to the theme that was already there in *The Wardrobe*. There was in that tale the infamous knife attack, but there was good reason for this. With the urge to confess now grows a parallel urge to justify. Perhaps it is uncivilized for blood to flow, but is this really an offence against culture? Civilization, according to Mann's 'Wartime Thoughts', is only reason, enlightenment, good behaviour, only spirit and the enemy of the drives, the passions'. Culture, on the other hand, the highest value, may be 'bloody and fearful', it embraces 'pederasty, ritual cruelty, human sacrifice'[56], i.e. more or less what occurs in the boundless mingling of the dream orgies.

It is remarkable how Thomas Mann returns from this general reflection back to the personal. Quite in the spirit of Aschenbach he compares art and war, the soldier and the artist, who have so much in common: organization, the mutual influence of enthusiasm and order, solidity, precision, and so on for a further half page, on which one phrase alone is italicized, evidently the decisive thing that the artist shares with the warrior, the *testimony of blood*.

This is from 1915, a time when many writers composed a lot of overheated nonsense about war and blood. But Mann's persistence on this personal 'testimony of blood' did not alter when he changed sides and saw reason. In the republic speech of 1922, his subject in addressing the militarist youth was not just Walt Whitman's worship of boys. He is no lukewarm pacifist, he confesses: 'I know what blood is, what death, what comradeship.'[57]

Yet his war service was no more than the writing of his *Reflections*, and it was only ink that he spilled here.

ALONE TOGETHER

The 'testimony of blood' is also vouchsafed to the peaceful Hans Castorp, who travels to Davos for a three-week visit and remains there for seven years, which corresponds more or less to the way that the 'humorous companion-piece to *Death in Venice*'[58] grew into one of the great novels of world literature. That its subject is Eros, sickness and death has been repeated ad nauseam. But blood and violence? In this mystical-humouristic goldfish bowl[59] one doesn't expect to find morays or piranhas, nor do they in fact turn up. In this respect *The Magic Mountain* remains the pendant to the Venice story that Mann has planned: the bloody deed is shifted into unreality. At the centre of the novel the eager Castorp goes out into the mountains, where he is surprised by a snowstorm and in a state close to death has a double dream. First of all, his gaze reveals a landscape of lagoons and the Mediterranean, which he remembers even though he has never been to Greece or Sicily – or more specifically Naples.[60] Young people are playing on the beach, and the dreamer's heart goes out to them, even though he asks himself whether he does not make himself 'perhaps punishable'[61] by watching them. The suspicion is confirmed when one of the boys, a resurrection of Tadzio, signals to him with a serious expression. Castorp is thoroughly frightened, he turns away and finds himself before the pillars of a temple complex. A sculpture of mother and daughter makes him still more afraid, for some obscure reason. The door to the temple chamber is open, and his knees almost give way when he insistently glances inside; two grey-haired witches are tearing apart and devouring a child. Castorp sees 'bright hair blood-smeared'.[62] This primal scene, he recognizes in the dreamy reflections that follow, is connected with the southern idyll: the one does not exist without the other, the Apollonian sunny happiness is founded on the hideous crime, the 'blood-sacrifice' that underpins the solemn gaiety of the beach people.[63]

Just as in *Death in Venice*, everything in this double dream is strongly stereotyped, from the *locus amoenus* to the statue of

Demeter and Persephone. No longer does anything in it seem personal, and the lesson Castorp draws from it is an italicized message to humanity: '*For the sake of goodness and love, man shall let death have no sovereignty over his thoughts.*' Still, the foundation of the ethical imperative develops from the first-person 'I will'; it is a personal project of pacification.[64] He does not want to think always of death and hideousness, and elevates this wish into the idea of humanity, which however soon fades away. On his return to the sanatorium Castorp forgets the dream message completely.

This reverie however was not his first. The first of his dreams was that of his youthful flame Hippe. Castorp has ventured one excursion into the mountains already before the snowstorm. He leaves the sanatorium and heads into the unknown, but is in too much of a hurry; he feels giddy and lies down on a bank. Here he has a vision, a reverie, in which the gigantic wooden phallus revealed in Aschenbach's dream collapses into a propelling pencil. The vision of his schoolfriend Hippe, who lends him the ambiguous pencil, is the first scene in the novel in which eroticism is revealed to be homoeroticism. And the substance flows as it evidently must: Hans Castorp has a nosebleed when Hippe appears to him.

This blood gives the narrator the occasion for a rather too strong comparison. After his vision Castorp returns to the Berghof, where Krokowski's lecture has already begun. The audience scarcely notice him, and this is just as well, 'for he looked rather ghastly. His face white as a sheet, his coat spotted with blood – he might have been a murderer stealing from his crime.'[65] The murder theme continues its perambulations through the mouths of outsiders, after the model of Christian Buddenbrook. One of these successors to Christian is Ferdinand Wehsal from Mannheim, who takes a special interest in medieval torture racks and lies on one himself. If Haus Berghof had offered a rice diet, it would have done him good: the poor man lies on the rack of lust, he is consumed by his desire for Clavdia Chauchat, dreams every night that she spits at him or beats him, and he shares his sorrows with Hans Castorp. It is a human need to relieve the heart, he says to his more fortunate rival, and moans about the 'hellish disgrace' of his nights, using a good deal of material from the notebooks that Thomas Mann kept during the Ehrenberg time.[66] Madame Chauchat refuses him, but for what reason? 'What is it I want, Castorp? Do I want to kill her? Do I want to shed her blood? I only want to fondle her!'[67] Not every lover would have in mind this possibility of confusion. But it also slips into the discussions that Naphta has with Settembrini. They are arguing about the death penalty, which Naphta defends. His first argument still follows the teaching of Schopenhauer. Man is what he has willed to be, he neither can nor wants to be other, and this is precisely his guilt: 'He has revelled in slaying, and does not pay too dear in being slain. Let him die, then, for he has gratified his heart's deepest desire.' But this is more than the philosopher had to say. Settembrini is incredulous or indignant, and asks: 'Deepest desire?' 'Deepest desire,' Naphta repeats. An embarrassed cough. Wehsal, as is only to be expected, pulls a face. Settembrini cunningly remarks that there is a kind of generalization that has a distinctly personal cast. 'Have you ever had a desire to commit murder?' To which Naphta answers:

That is no concern of yours. But if I had, I should laugh in the face of any ignorant humanitarianism that tried to feed me on skilly till I died a natural death. It is absurd for the murderer to outlive the murdered. They two, alone together, as two beings are together in only one other human relationship, have, like them, the one acting, the other suffering him, shared a secret that binds them for ever together.[68]

A deep and heavy secret, to be sure. 'The one acting, the other suffering him' – a deliberate ambiguity between the sexual act and the murderer and his victim; just as in the fairy-tale of *The Wardrobe* where the question of gender is avoided when one person stabs a knife into the other.

Settembrini declared that 'he lacked the brains necessary to the understanding of this death-and-murder mysticism', and did not miss them either. Not so Thomas Mann, who, in a 1926 article on the death penalty, notes his agreement with Naphta as an 'unsympathetic friend', precisely referring to Naphta's lecture on the deepest pleasure. He cannot see the death penalty as completely evil, Mann writes, especially since in the *Reflections of a Nonpolitical Man* he had taken it upon himself to maintain 'that a humanity set on doing life out of all its heavy, deadly serious aspects and pursuing its own unmanning, its castration, such a humanity is not mine, nor what I would desire'.[69] Which means that killing can indeed be the deepest pleasure and that it amounts to castration – a strikingly chosen word – to renounce this; and furthermore that Mann, when he says 'heavy', does indeed mean something deadly serious.

At the end, however, he pronounces himself, like Settembrini, against the death penalty. For this surprising turn he relies on Sigmund Freud, quoting from his 'splendid treatment' *Totem and Taboo* the passage in which Freud indicates the similarity of forbidden stimuli in the criminal and the revenging society. 'There you have it, hypocrites!' Mann concludes, and declares himself against the 'fascist truth' that knowledge should never hinder will, deed and passion.[70]

It is still, for all that, a truth, even if a fascist one, which from this point Mann therefore opposes. In 1943 Thomas Mann wrote a preface – 'Tables of the Law' – to a volume titled *The Ten Commandments*, designed to show how Nazism had perverted these. Mann describes here the imposition of these commandments, and the man Moses who converts his obstinate people. Again it is Freud whom he turns to for counsel – and once again the not completely evil Naphta is in the wings.

In his celebrated essay on Moses, Freud had reiterated his thesis from *Totem and Taboo* about the origin of morality and religion. At the beginning was the killing of the father; the formation of conscience derives from a primal crime, from a murder.[71] In Thomas Mann's account, this principle is reiterated, but with a specifically personal mark. His relationship to the main character is more personal than might be thought. 'Increasingly desirous of influencing the people,' he notes in his diary before he embarks on Freud's *Moses and Monotheism* (28 April 1939). Just like his other heroes, the author of *The Ten Commandments* is also an autobiographical figure, a reflection of the man who has to address his stubborn people and hammer moral concepts into them. This reflection is apparent even in Moses's outward form. A not so distant model would be Michelangelo's statue, but how does Mann visualize the author of the tablets? Just like the man-loving sculptor himself, the forceful Michelangelo who wrestles for the spiritual under his pressing sensuality, and to whom Mann was to devote a late and impassioned essay, in which he speaks almost without conceal-ment of himself and his sorrow over Franz Westermeier.

We learn in the very first sentence how this Moses, with so personal a mark on his head, had a very unusual birth. This differs from Freud's supposition, in which Moses was an Egyptian, and prolongs the series of artists who, like Tonio Kröger, have felt mixed blood in their veins. The second sentence gives us the fol-lowing information: 'Early on he killed in a frenzy; therefore he knew better than the inexperienced that, though killing is delec-table, *having* killed is detestable; he knew you should not kill.'[72] The creation of culture is the fruit of an early misdeed. The law is devised and championed not by an innocent, but by the man who has tasted guilt. He has an inner affinity to what he combats; Moses, tracing the letters of the Decalogue with his own blood, repeats this in symbolic miniature.

Thomas Mann did not simply dream this up. His source is the second book of Moses, Exodus 2: 11–12:

One day when Moses was grown up, he went out to his own kinsmen and saw them at their heavy labour. He saw an Egypt-ian strike one of his fellow-Hebrews. He looked this way and that, and, seeing there was no one about, he struck the Egypt-ian down and hid his body in the sand.

What is noteworthy about Mann's version is the little reinterpretation. The biblical Moses evidently acts not in a blaze of fury, but rather, in the literal sense, with circumspection. He looks this way and that, and makes sure that no one can spy on his deed. If he had been seen, he would have been able to leave off. And the Bible says neither that he finds this delectable nor that he is subsequently plagued by remorse.

As we shall note, Thomas Mann always deviates from the source when he is drawn back to his original story. The source may even be something recently experienced, which he leads round to the lethal theme. This is the case with the story *Mario and the Magician*, which like *Death in Venice* was sparked by a vacation in Italy – notoriously dangerous as these now were. In September 1926 Mann spent two weeks with his family at Forte dei Marmi; apart from the unpleasant impressions of a hysterical national mood, he also brought back home the memory of the performance of a well-known hypnotist. Three years later, after these memories had sufficiently fermented, he wrote the story that was to be one of his best, and in which it is not hard to recognize the old theme. *Mario and the Magician* ends, like *The Wardrobe*, with a murder, and in this case too there are good reasons for it. The hypnotist Cipolla, to whom Mann lends his own private nickname of 'Magician', exposes Mario, whom he signals up onto the stage with his index finger, to a fatal erotic humiliation. The magician leads Mario to believe that he is the girl with whom Mario is in love:

'Kiss me!' said the hunchback. 'Trust me, I love thee. Kiss me here.' And with the tip of his index finger, hand, arm, and little finger outspread, he pointed to his cheek, near the mouth. And Mario bent and kissed him.[73]

This has its fatal results. After Cipolla has woken him with a crack of the whip, Mario presses his hands to his abused lips and storms down the steps: 'Once below, and even while in full retreat, Mario hurled himself round with legs flung wide apart; one arm flew up, and two flat shattering detonations crashed through applause and laughter.'[74] The enforced kiss between two men leads to the revenge of the humiliated party: Mario shoots the seducer who exposed him.

This ending is no longer drawn from a holiday experience in Il Duce's Italy. Everything was as he had depicted it, except for the deadly shots and the love intrigue. It was precisely for the sake of this invented finale, however, that Mann had written the whole story, as he explains in a letter. The lethal ending, the shooting, was an idea of Erika's[75] and set everything else in motion; he would otherwise have had no impulse to tell the story, 'and if you say, without the hotelier I would have left Cipolla alive, the real truth is exactly the reverse: in order to kill Cipolla, I needed the hotelier – and the rest of the preparatory annoyances'.[76]

The desire that leads to a bloody deed is also the theme of the Indian novel written in 1940, The Transposed Heads. The themes from the early work that return again here – the stabbings from Tobias Mindernickel and The Wardrobe, the suicide from Little Herr Friedemann – blossom unexpectedly in this exotic air. The realm of eighteen-armed Kali is not for the squeamish; this story, whose graphicness is surpassed only by the superb sense of comic detail

Mann has by now achieved, swims in blood as much as the goddess of desire and death herself: 'Blood steamed hot in the skull she held with one hand to her lips, and blood was at her feet in a spreading pool.'[77] This is the horror that confronts the frail sage when he enters the temple which has become the scene of the grisly event. The sage is named Shridaman (only one 'n'), and because his wife, the beautiful Sita, desires the strong-bodied Nanda, in full view of the goddess Kali, with his sex aroused in despair, he seizes the sharp-cutting sword and separates his head from his torso. His blood flows wild and fast, like that of his friend Nanda, who follows him into the shrine and, when he realizes what has been done, likewise hacks off his own head.

This is the same mythologically enhanced temple-and-sacrifice scene familiar from *The Magic Mountain*. And the obscene symbol from Aschenbach's dream is here as well: inside the temple loom the 'linga stones' which unobtrusively the two men touch before they draw their swords.[78] Kali in the end shows herself merciful and permits a restoration, which Sita uses for a transposition that leaves Shridaman's head on the powerful body of Nanda. But their pleasure is brief; at the end the newly joined stab each other, and Sita steps onto the pyre.

The 'productive terror' that the Indian material generated had already been detected by Thomas Mann's Goethe who, in the seventh chapter of *Lotte in Weimar*, reflects about seduction as the 'paradigm of all temptation and guilt'. The poem that Goethe wants to make of the pariah story, of the seduced Brahmin woman and the severed and transposed heads, he had found in some old tome. 'Make a poem of this!' he and Mann instruct themselves.[79]

The 'autobiographical urge' that Goethe has to justify in his solilo-quy[80] is that of Thomas Mann throughout the whole novel. Seduction by one's own sex appears to Goethe as the revenge of narcissism;[81] revenge is linked as ever with seduction; cruelty is for him the main ingredient of love,[82] the ego a 'sword-dance of difficulty';[83] he finds his own existence murderous;[84] and even Lotte, in the carriage conversation that proceeds in the same open way as that between Krull and Rosza, speaks to him of 'human sacrifice'.[85] With all this, Mann has not stepped one foot away from his innermost thematic circle.

SHECHEM

As the Indian legend was simply an offshoot of the Goethe novel, this in its turn was a mere insertion into the tetralogy *Joseph and His Brothers*. This masterpiece in humorous vein, which occupied Thomas Mann for almost two decades, appears at first sight free from the compulsive motif. But this first sight could not be more deceptive. On closer inspection it is striking to discover how in all four books the lines of force run towards scenes that once again tell the old business, the tale of voluptuousness and hot guilt. Let us consider the series more closely.

The first book in the tetralogy deals with *The Tales of Jacob*, the bloodiest of which is the story of Shechem – a fortified city which Jacob's sons, who had already acquired land in the region, were keen to attack, needing only a pretext for this. They find this pre-text in their sister Dinah, whose charms make the son of the city's lord a second Wehsal. This Dinah is no beauty, but irresistible;

her aura even overspills the bounds of one novel. Before this son and heir she had already seduced Felix Krull: with her long, sinister-sweet and sometimes squinting eyes, her snub nose, her broad, red, upturned mouth and her petite breasts, she is the spitting image of the bad love teacher.[86] Without Dinah, the Khabir maid, complains the son and heir, his body will rot. When he appeals to Jacob for her, and offers rich wedding gifts, it is explained that first of all he must have himself circumcised. A week later, radiant if still weak, he returns to collect his hoped-for reward. Certainly, he is told, he has been circumcised, but with a metal knife, not a stone one, so this is not valid. When he then loses patience and abducts Dinah, he actually falls in with the brothers' secret wish. After consummation the son and heir returns for reconciliation, but the brothers then demand that all the men of the city must be circumcised, and with stone knives, then there can be a wedding with laughter and tears. Three nights later, when the men of the city are still lying in pain and changing their bandages, the brothers fall on the city and carry out a frightful butchery. The inhabitants without exception are massacred with fire and sword, alleys and houses are awash with blood, the son and heir is placed 'shamefully disfigured, stuck head-down in the waste-pipe of his own latrine'.[87] This 'bloody marriage feast'[88] is the original crime that is alluded to over and again in the subsequent volumes, until the late marriage of Joseph gives the author occasion for a long reflection on the affinity between wedding and death, the theft of virginity and murder.[89]

The attack on Shechem, if not its sadistic details, is familiar from the Bible. The fate of Dinah, however, is an invention of

Thomas Mann. Different from the original, and also contrary to
how he initially presents it — for his Dinah has nothing against
lying with the son and heir — the ostensible reason the brothers
give for their butchery is that their sister was 'violated' and had to
be rescued from the 'lustful Sodomites'.[90] Here, in the spiteful
exaggeration of the brothers, we glimpse once only, in the whole
of Mann's work, the explicit name of that hidden event: a homosexual violation leading to bloody revenge.

But this subject also recurs in the following volume *Young
Joseph*, which likewise relates a bloody deed. Insulted by Joseph's
boastful dreams of elevation, the brothers abandon Shechem. At
Jacob's command Joseph travels after them, and what happens
next we know from the Bible: the brothers throw him into a pit.
How is this related in Thomas Mann's version?

Here Joseph approaches the brothers' camp in the veiled
wedding-dress of his dead mother Rachel. As soon as they see
him they attack him:

> They fell upon him as a pack of hungry wolves falls upon the
> prey; their blood-blinded lust knew no pause or consideration
> [. . .] 'Down, down, down!' they panted with one voice; it was
> the *ketonet* they meant, the picture-robe, the veil. It must come
> off.[91]

They undress him and tear his veil, and his garland of myrtle is
soon lying torn in the moss. These are metaphors of deflowering
or rape. Indeed, a more direct expression is soon used:

Desperately he tried to protect the garment and keep the remnants and ruins of it still upon him. Several times he cried out: 'My coat! My coat!' and even after he stood naked, still begged them: 'Don't tear it!', as if fearing for his virginity.[92]

Why does Mann introduce virginity here? In order to rule out the slightest doubt as to what he has in mind, he sums up once again what happened to Joseph, as it had previously to Dinah: 'As love unveils the bride in the bedchamber, thus had their fury done to him, and they had known him naked, so that his frame quivered with the deathly shame.'[93]

Even in *Felix Krull* the verb 'know' is unmistakable,[94] in a biblical epic it is quite unambiguous: Joseph fell victim to a gang rape, with a deadly blow only just prevented. As if to show that, after already indicating so much, he could now actually call the thing by its bare name, Thomas Mann returns to it once again. He lists the reasons for Joseph's chastity; one of these is the caution 'which the experience of frightful violation, the tearing of his wreath and robe, must have strengthened mightily'.[95] It need scarcely be spelled out that the wreath is not torn without blood; in winding streams this runs down Joseph's body, spilled by his brothers' rage, a body that was so exquisitely tender to their untender contact that the malefactors brooded over it for a long while after they had finished their work.[96]

When they took counsel after this first explosion, little would have lacked for them to bump Joseph off altogether. As in both *Tobias Mindernickel* and *Felix Krull* – in the latter case on an occasion that only Naphta would perceive as akin[97] – the narrator refuses to go into too coarse a detail: 'I would fain pass over what was said next, for it would shock our modern taste.'[98] Even so, we learn that the sturdy Gad proposes to run his knife through Joseph's throat, 'as Jacob had done with the kid', and Tobias Mindernickel to his dog Esau. Thanks to Reuben's intervention, Joseph's fate was moderated to being thrown in the pit, though even so Joseph feels compassion 'for his murderers'.[99] When, in a narrow escape, he is freed from the pit, it is Judah who comes to his aid. Joseph is sold to the Ishmaelites for twenty pieces of silver (though they don't pay cash for him, but 'a great many knives and trinkets').[100] When they have sent Jacob the robe smeared with an animal's blood, the brothers swear an oath of silence, designed to bind and tie them, as if they were not distinct people, 'but one man who presseth his lips together and openeth them not, but rather dieth, his mouth shut together over his secret'.[101]

Joseph, meanwhile, travels with the Ishmaelites into Egypt, and is sold to the house of Potiphar, where throughout the third volume in the series – *Joseph in Egypt* – he works at his ascent and struggles against the attractions of Potiphar's wife. Married to a eunuch, this Mut-em-inet, whose desire is awakened by Joseph's beauty, pleads with him ever more forcefully to still her blood, and finally resorts to action. First she entices him, then she threatens him with exotic tortures if he will not sleep with her,[102] tortures whose depiction caused their inventor, according to a passage in his diary, sexual excitement (29 May 1936).[103] When even these threats prove ineffective, Mut-em-inet loses her last inhibitions and tells everyone around her pangs of love. A group of ladies, whom she craftily manipulates, are to give her words material expression. The important instruments here are the fruit-knives which she has had so thoroughly whetted that they are as sharp as razors. These little knives are found next to the blood-oranges that are being peeled by the ladies of the household, when Joseph enters and attracts the glances of all. They stare at him with desire, and what happens then is exactly what Mut-em-inet had in mind:

> It was a fearful sight. With some the nimble knife had gone an inch deep in the flesh and blood did not ooze, it spouted. The little hands, the golden apples, were drenched with the red liquid, it dyed the fresh whiteness of the linen garments and soaked through into the women's laps, making pools which dripped down on the floor and their little feet.[104]

There was lust, so blood must flow; the principle is so powerful that it finds expression in the smallest details.

Mut-em-inet, who becomes ever more of a maenad, finally resorts to the ultimate means. She conspires in witchcraft with the old hag Tabubu, who agrees to deliver the stubborn man to her. Tabubu calls on the assistance of an obscure goddess, known as 'the bitch'; a living dog is also needed for the ceremony. Given Esau's fate, it is not hard to suspect what will happen to it. This time the narrator does not refrain from going into detail:

> 'Where is the double-edged blade? To hand. And the cur? It lies on the floor, like a young hyena, with chains on its claws, and with moist muzzle bound [. . .]' 'Bring him on, then, the

sniffling cur, the obscene beast, and slit his throat! Slit his belly open and bathe your hands in the smoking entrails as they steam up into the cool moonlighted night. Smeared with blood, dripping with entrails, I hold them up to you, my hands, for I have made them in your image.'[105]

The ritual slaughter, at the hands of witches or Bacchae – as we had in the dream scenes – serves bodily pleasure. The soul, to Mut-em-inet's sorrow, remains turned away. Just as Tonio Kröger in his descent into sensuality and burning guilt suffered 'unspeakably', so Mut-em-inet likewise, at the end of the ritual, complains to the purer spirits how sad this vileness makes her. Tabubu, however, is still brazen after all this excess, and addresses her with contempt, which gives the narrator the occasion for the following sentence:

> That is a very old human experience: that when a man is tempted to fall below his better self, his tempters, those who drag him down, alarm him and mock him when they have him safely below, by the insolence with which they suddenly speak of his new and unfamiliar state.

As Settembrini rightly observed, there is a way of generalizing that gives the subject a personal colour. And more personal still is the sentence that follows:

> Pride demands that he conceal his fear and bewilderment, that he answer them: 'Let things be as they are, I knew what I did

when I resolved to follow you.' And in such a way did Mut express herself.[106]

By following the seducer, Mut-em-inet approaches close to the goal of her desire: the erection that she catches a glimpse of when Joseph escapes her by the skin of his teeth. When Joseph flees from the love-crazed woman he is revealed as a rampant ass – 'his flesh stood up against his spirit'[107] – yet even so he remains steadfast. He is the lucky hero of the fairy-tale who resists the two things, seduction and violence, or more precisely, the seduction to violence offered him by Mut-em-inet in a lisping childish voice. Thomas Mann has added to the biblical account that Mut-em-inet proposed Joseph should murder Potiphar:

'So, sweet Osarsiph, let us make him cold, for it is a little thing. [. . .] For you are right, my divine boy, to say that he stands in the way of our joy and we may do naught to him – you are right in your misgiving. But just therefore must you see that we must make him cold and send him out of this world, that the misgiving may be satisfied and we do him no more harm in our embracing. Do you understand, my little one?'[108]

Joseph replies that this is repugnant to him; all that is lacking is for her to say they would be accomplices together, as she gave him the idea and now unfortunately it is also his.

The fourth book – *Joseph the Provider* – deals at last with the great secret and its revelation, when after his second fall Joseph becomes Pharaoh's right-hand man and as governor of Egypt receives his brothers who are suffering from the corn famine. The climax of this final volume is Judah's great speech of confession, in which he breaks the brothers' fearsome oath and admits to the governor their original crime.

It had already dawned on the sons of Jacob quite a bit earlier that all the governor's remarkable measures, as well as the plague and the accusation of their being spies, were 'punishment for long past guilt'.[109] And Judah was the first to suspect that the secret that underlies all this could only be explained by revealing another secret.[110] In their hour of distress, when they stand accused before Pharaoh's representative, Judah's heart revolts, he delivers the novel's great speech, and breaks the oath in two over his knee: the eleventh son, his father's lamb, was not torn to pieces by a wild animal, but sold by his brothers into slavery. 'He stood weaving to and fro. The brothers had gone pale; yet they were deeply relieved that the secret was out at last.'[111]

At the climax of this final book, if not before, Judah proves to have been a major character in the novel, long undervalued. Judah is the shadow of Joseph, the dark chosen one on whom Thomas Mann conveys everything that he elsewhere deposited onto Wehsal or the hallucinating Christian. He would later thank a reviewer of *Doctor Faustus* for pointing out 'the parallel between Adrian and Judah'.[112] There are three characteristics that he endows him with, and all are related. All three would be familiar to us even if all we had of Thomas Mann was his speeches, letters and diaries; they form the inner triumvirate of his artistic existence.

The first of these three is the suffering that goes with desire. Judah's 'sex life had from the first been marked by disorder and suffering. His relationship with the love-goddess kept him strained and unsatisfied, he writhed under her lash and was her unsubmissive slave – hence the deep conflict in his soul and the lack of unity in his character.'[113] But after Judah and his brothers had got rid of Joseph, Ashtaroth had intensified her plaguing; it has to be said 'since that time the man had atoned in hell – in one of the hells there are, the hell of sex'.[114]

Judah sees this as punishment for his old misdeed. And this is the second of his characteristics, the sense of guilt, blame, duty, corresponding to an equally strong need for purity. Just like Christian Buddenbrook he is caught up in an act of violence, and though far from the worst of the brothers in this respect, he is certainly the most sensitive. He is the only one to be dreadfully upset by the act, which gnaws at his conscience.[115] And for this reason – the third characteristic – his spirit develops. Judah delivers the brave speech because he 'had familiar knowledge of sin and guilt, and therefore he could fitly represent the brothers. For guilt creates spirit, and the other way round: without spirit there is no guilt at all.'[116]

This is just one of such sentences, with both a general and a personal stamp, that Judah leaves in his wake as he proceeds through the text. Time and again the narrator uses him as an occasion to speak of the nature of guilt. Even as a child, Judah is inflamed against the still unborn Joseph; Leah places the kernel of hatred in the brothers' hearts, and the narrator raises the question whether the brothers could not simply have come to terms with each other. His answer is not surprising, Mann has already prepared his line of argument in his reflections on culture versus civilization:

Very much happens in the world; and as we cannot wish that it might rather have peacefully remained unhappened, we may not curse the passions which are its instrument; for without passion and guilt nothing could proceed.[117]

This is even before the crime that also drives Judah forward, precisely because he always has it in mind. The barb of the bad conscience sharpens the moral sense. It should not be thought that the guilty one is immoral, quite the opposite. The narrator instructs us that 'sinners can be extremely sensitive to the sins of the world,'[118] and has Judah declare, about the silver beaker hidden in his brother's pack: 'I do not say we are innocents, that would be sacrilege. But there is guilt and guilt, and maybe guilt is prouder than innocence is; anyhow, to nab silver cups is not in our line.'[119] The dignity of guilt: this is the halo on Judah's head, the single thought of this character that underlies his very existence. In a further aside the narrator informs us yet again:

Only the thick-witted should commit crimes; they do not mind, they live from day to day and nothing worries them. Evil is for the dull-witted; anyone with even traces of sensibility should avoid it if he possibly can, for he will have to smart for it. That he has a conscience makes him worse off than ever; he will be punished precisely on account of his conscience.[120]

In Judah's case, conscience does not just lead to his seeing all the misfortune that he suffers 'as retaliation [. . .] for what he committed, what he was involved in committing', it also means that he understands this misfortune as an honour: 'he would have it that he was suffering punishment, he alone, and looked with contempt on those who, thanks to their thick skin, remained unscathed. Such is the particular arrogance of conscience.'[121] A conclusion that clearly expresses the particular tone of 'I know what I'm speaking about'.

But why does Thomas Mann choose Judah for this guilt complex, why not Joseph, why not Reuben or Zebulun? Because it is Judah who receives the blessing. Not Joseph, the fortunate one, who escaped the bloody act, but Judah, the sinner, tormented by his feeling of guilt and driven into spiritual development.

This introduces the theme that dominates the late novels of Thomas Mann: elevation despite guilt, elevation precisely because of guilt. It is a theme that grew important to him only with his worldwide celebrity; no longer would the laurel crown be just a crazy dream. From *Joseph* on, it drives out everything else: Leverkühn, allied with the Devil, ends as the lamb of God and Messiah of art; the Holy Sinner, who combines in himself all the horrors of sin, becomes the head of Christianity. And on each occasion we have a speech of confession and acknowledgement such as Judah delivers before Joseph. Each time, moreover, the guilt is precisely named.

PALE MAN, CONFESSING

In *The Holy Sinner*, one might believe, the guilt in question is the sin of incest: that is how the story's material is presented. The original guilt however is something other, which no source discloses.[122] In reporting what took place, the good narrator-monk Clemens has to overcome his own disgust: the bedchamber of brother and sister is 'so full of tenderness, defilement, rage, and blood and sin that my heart turns over for pity, shame, and anguish and I may scarcely tell it all'.[123] The defilement we know from the legend of Gregory, but the blood and rage? In *The Holy Sinner* something happens before the incest, something one might seek in vain in the medieval source of Hartmann von Aue. The dog Hanegiff is in the chamber of the excited pair and howls painfully:

> And the younker just as he was, half crazed, sprang out of bed for his hunting-knife, seized the dog, and cut his throat, so that with a throat-rattle he stretched his limbs in death; threw the knife on the body, whose blood the sand of the floor drank up; then he turned drunkenly back to the place of another shame.
>
> Oh woe for the good and lovely dog! To my mind it was the worst that happened that night, I rather pardon the rest, unlawful as it was. But I suppose it was all of one piece and was not more blameworthy here than there: a spewing of love, murder and passion of the flesh, that may God pity.[124]

A spewing, in fact, that had proceeded through Thomas Mann's work ever since Tobias Mindernickel stabbed poor Esau. The original sin is the murder that precedes the act of desire, not the incest that sets the powerful apparatus of mercy in motion; Clemens leaves as little doubt about this as does the bride and mother of the new pope, who in her final confession expressly remembers the howling Hanegiff.[125]

A second if putative murder corresponds to this first one, and this does have its prototype in Hartmann von Aue. After the incest with his mother is discovered, Grigorss seeks a wasteland where he can atone and takes his rest in a fisherman's hut. This fisherman, jealous of the handsome ascetic, sets him down as he wished on an island and chains him with a leg-iron, the key to which he throws in the sea. Seventeen years pass. Against all expectation Grigorss survives on his rock, and in Rome two people dream of a newly chosen pope. These two dreamer-emissaries set out to find him and stumble on the old hut. What they, and the reader, are seeking is Grigorss on his stone; no one has asked about the situation of the ill-willed fisherman. In Hartmann von Aue he has completely forgotten the incident.[126] Not so in Thomas Mann, who affords us a glance into his soul:

> I will add that the man did not in the least want to remember the visit and shoved it out of his mind as much as possible. For in retrospect it always seemed to him, though actually he had at that time done just what the strange man wanted, as though he had committed something like a crime – in short, a murder. And one would rather banish such ideas.[127]

This kind of thing one *would rather* banish, but does not succeed in doing so. The fisherman, for his part, 'did not succeed badly, so far as the upper layer of his consciousness went'. The lower layer, however, sees to it that he betrays himself as soon as the emissaries from Rome arrive. He claims not to have sent anyone away from his door, whether 'lord or beggar',[128] but when the key to the leg-iron turns up in the belly of the pike that he serves up to them, Thomas Mann has him where he wants him: 'Then the blenched man straightened and made his confession.'[129] He is pale as the brothers were at Judah's revelation, pale as Adrian Leverkühn in his final address, whose admissions were recorded by his friend Zeitblom in *Doctor Faustus*, his pen already trembling as he sits down to write – a tremble that he shares with his author.

No other book so exhausted Thomas Mann as *Doctor Faustus*, this 'radical confession', this 'confession of a life' and 'transformed autobiography', which he wrote in a 'state of profound excitement, deep turbulence and surrender' and with such a determined 'investment of reality and a life's secret' that the 'idea of making public this work of life and its secrecy' remained 'in the depths of my soul something strange and unfathomable' – 'the whole thing is like an open wound'.[130] There can be no doubt about it: if there is one work to which Thomas Mann confided, in however coded a form, the secrets whose discovery he feared in April 1933 as a mortal danger, then this work is *Doctor Faustus*. And vice versa; what else should the secret work deal with if not precisely those secrets of his life that the diary passage mentions?

This however is almost the only sure thing that one can say about this most intricate of his novels, in which allusions are piled one above the other like the mattresses and eiderdowns in the tale of the princess who still feels the pea underneath. And at the deepest point beneath the layers of allusion there is concealed here, too, the hard nub that robbed the author of his sleep and sorely pressed on his soul.

Is this nub the affair with Schwerdtfeger, whom Adrian

addresses in the familiar form after they have spent a holiday together – in short, the story of Mann's youthful passion for Paul Ehrenberg? But something is no longer a secret if it is bruited about at every opportunity. All that was needed was the inquiry of an acquaintance, and Mann burst out:

> Ah, those friends of my youth, the Ehrenbergs! Carl, who wrote you the stupid letter, played *Tristan* with such legato, and 'that Paul', who was certainly a painter, like so very many, but an attractive lad and indeed one of my great passions – I cannot put it otherwise.[131]

No one forced this incriminating word out of him. And no one could overlook, in reading *The Genesis of a Novel*, how in *Doctor Faustus* 'the homosexual element plays an impish role' in the relationship between Adrian and Rudi Schwerdtfeger.[132]

Is it then the guilt of the cold, egocentric artist that Mann demonizes in the figure of Leverkühn? This is certain enough, also that Mann suffered from it, yet for that very reason this cannot be the secret: in *The Genesis of a Novel* Mann speaks quite openly of a 'colouring of existence by this sense of guilt', bearing on his 'inhumanity based on absentmindedness'.[133] Perhaps the question should rather be posed the other way round: what can these secrets not be, what is open to view in these layers of allusion?

Let us suppose that *Faustus* was relieved of all those passages where a well-annotated edition would indicate a source, whether another text, a work of plastic art or a transmitted biographical detail. It would be possible in this way to remove page after page:

references to the medieval *Faust-Buch* and the life of Nietzsche, to Luther and the engravings of Dürer, to the twelve-tone doctrine and Adorno's musical theory, to Frau von Meck and the composer Alban Berg; to Kierkegaard and the tales of Hans Christian Andersen, to Reisiger, Preetorius and Mann's grandson Frido, to the suicide of his sister Carla, the triangular wooing from Shakespeare's comedies, the tramcar murder from a press clipping, Mahler's *Kindertotenlieder*, the mental breakdowns of Schumann and Hugo Wolf, Dante's *Inferno* and Michelangelo's *Last Judgement*.

Not a lot would remain if all these pages were removed. The novel has no page free of such references, and reveals its 'bloody radicalism'[134] in its citative style. But there would be a few passages without references, and there are quotations which, as in 'Tables of the Law', the *Joseph* novels and *The Holy Sinner*, undergo a small but decisive alteration.

The original story that triggers off all the others is taken from Paul Deussen's *Erinnerungen an Friedrich Nietzsche* and the account of the philosopher's sickness in Jena. On his arrival in Leipzig, Leverkühn is enticed by a city guide into a house of pleasure where he suffers 'the trauma of encounter with the soulless drive': caressed by Hetaera Esmeralda whom he flees from but who, a year later, when he follows her to Pressburg, specifically infects him.[135]

But this is not quite how it was in the Nietzsche tradition. There the arrogant man is not caressed by an arm – a contact that Zeitblom traces the whole day on his own cheek[136] – and there he doesn't follow after the dark-haired woman, but simply 'returns to a place of that kind', as Thomas Mann himself puts it.[137] The long journey and the fixation is new – although the model for the fixation has long been familiar to us. Hetaera Esmeralda wears a little jacket like Dürer's 'Negress Katharina'; but with her 'big gam, snub nose, almond eyes'[138] she is strongly reminiscent of Rosza, the earliest seductress in *Felix Krull*, who for her part conjures up the portrait that the young Thomas Mann gave of Naples. The origin of the corrupter is taken not from Nietzsche's life but from that of Felix Krull. Rosza is a Hungarian, and this is where Leverkühn pursues the dark lady, to enjoy her poisoned flesh. Hungary is likewise the origin of Adrian's invisible patron Frau von Tolna, a reapparition of the mysterious hetaera.[139]

Esmeralda has a pimp, and he too is an old acquaintance, to be sought in vain in other sources. The 'losel' in Adrian's conversation with the Devil, the weedy, pale red-head with a cap on his head and his tongue in the corner of his mouth, is the equivalent of both the Neapolitan pimp-comedian from *Death in Venice*, and the Municher Strolch from *The Hungry*; as his actor's voice shows, he too is from the dramatic profession.[140] His entrance is also familiar to us: suddenly he is sitting on the sofa, in the stone hall in Palestrina, and any doubt about his actual existence he declares to be 'pure hypochondria'.[141] Quite rightly, as we know, for the beginning of the scene relates to a visionary experience. Christian Buddenbrook speaks of him, as he spoke of the drawn knives in the south: knives which in *Faustus* become the symbolic knives of the little mermaid, whose pains her lover must also suffer.

Adrian may have contact with her – or with him, as she conceals the Devil within – but he must not love her, this is what the cheesy hoodlum teaches him at the end of the discussion. They are in business together, as attested by his blood, which means that he will achieve a 'breakthrough' with ensuing success and fame, but at the price of a ban on love.[142]

The consequences of this ban are the two crimes that run through the novel from its very beginning. The first is the death of the child, for which Leverkühn feels responsible. Apart from an allusion to the tragedy of Gustav Mahler, who lost his beloved daughter after he wrote the *Kindertotenlieder*, this part of the action is poorly sourced. 'What a sin, what a crime,' Leverkühn laments when his nephew dies; but where exactly does his guilt lie, except that he uses Echo as inspiration (as Mann did with his grandson Frido, whose depiction goes beyond the many 'murders' that Mann acknowledged to his wife and put quotation marks around in his diaries)?[143] The logic of myth requires the Devil to carry off the boy, since Leverkühn loves him impermissibly. This 'impermissible' passes into ambiguity, when Leverkühn accuses himself of having feasted his eyes on the boy and exposed him to 'poisonous influences'.[144] Removed from its context, this could describe the uncle as a wicked paedophile – but only if removed in this way. There is an abyss, if indeed a narrow one, between the love of Leverkühn for Echo and paedophilia – which is precisely why the author defended himself so sternly against a doctoral student who made too free with the traces of homosexuality. He can admit something here and there, says Mann, but the epiphany of the heavenly child is something that the researcher 'should not impugn, however "gently"'.[145]

There was not much to admit, since it lay open to view, in the second case in which Leverkühn breached the ban on love. The persistent courting of Schwerdtfeger reaches its goal in Hungary, after which Adrian addresses him with the familiar *Du*. But he takes revenge on Schwerdtfeger for coming too close. Zeitblom indicates this right at the beginning, and later speaks of the catastrophe in which Adrian is 'involved and active in an obscure and fatal way'.[146] Adrian sends Schwerdtfeger out as a suitor, but he woos successfully for himself. This is the theme of triangular wooing from the Shakespeare plays that Adrian sets to music. In Thomas Mann's account the theme undergoes a decisive extension: the betrayed one steers the too forceful party to his death. Schwerdtfeger's former beloved shoots him out of jealousy, before he can marry the woman intended for Adrian. The intrigue is convoluted enough, but its meaning is clear. 'Certainly I am changing this,' Thomas Mann wrote of his adaptation of Shakespeare: 'Adrian kills the friend whom he loves.'[147]

He changes it into something for which there is no source. But this change comes *before* the quotation. Shakespeare is the cover, and only secondary. The core of the plan is revealed in an early working note: 'He is forced to make use of his desire for marriage precisely to kill the person whom he had sex with.'[148] And so he sends Schwerdtfeger off to get shot in a tramcar.

Many readers of *Doctor Faustus* found this course of events unconvincing, so Mann frequently had to explain it. It strongly irritated his son Michael. In the Lübeck birthday speech on the *felix culpa*, Michael answered as follows the question as to how far a 'transformed autobiography' was actually involved in the collapse of spiritual arrogance into barbarism, which was the presupposition of fascism and the sin of Leverkühn: 'the implications cannot be thought through to the end'. What was certain, however, was 'that the narrator shared heavily in the guilt of the "friend" that he portrays here'.[149]

If Thomas Mann shared heavily in this, then what was transposed from life into fiction also had something relieving about it. 'This gloomy and radical work first had to be written, if I wanted to offer myself completely,' he said in a letter, and gave two examples of what the *Joseph* novels still did not contain: the epiphany of the child and 'Adrian's final confession of his life and sins'.[150]

In this ultimate confession, the climax of the novel that Thomas Mann also saw as his own testament, the man of sorrows Leverkühn, whose time has run out, confesses his series of sins.[151] His listeners first of all take this as art, as fiction. But quite wrongly: 'This was dead sober earnest, a confession, the truth, to listen to which a man in extreme agony of soul had called together his fellow-men', who for their part of course respond to this truth, 'when they could no longer consider it as poetry', with cold terror.[152] It is this 'bareness and baldness of unmediated revelation' that so vexes Zeitblom and causes him to hold high the protective vagueness of art.[153]

The confessor sits there pale as death, and admits the pact with the Devil that 'some kind of deed' had been sufficient to seal; he admits that he pursued the dark woman, that he poisoned the boy with his glances and that the Devil not only forbade him to marry, but also denied him the love for the man that he addressed as *Du*: 'So he forced me to use precisely this intent, that I coldly murdered the trusting one and will have confessed it today and here before you all, that I sit before you also as murtherer.'[154]

The confession is followed by a collapse and decline on the lines of Nietzsche. But before this point is reached, hope springs for a last time. Leverkühn had completed his work by way of murder and sexual abuse, and he only hopes that this work, created in misdeed, can mercifully turn out good. Perhaps God will take into account that he let himself grow sour, and count it in his favour that he 'obstinately finished all'.[155] Who here is speaking exclusively for himself is scarcely concealed any longer – for who else could raise this hope? Certainly not Leverkühn, whose pact with the Devil expressly relieved him of this very worry, so that he did not need to piece his work together half a page each morning, but either lay fallow like death or, in waves of overwhelming inspiration, shivering in holy terror, in a night kept from darkness by incessant lightning, could scarcely write down the inspirations that flooded over him.[156] With this kind of artistic creation there can be no talk of a work ethic of obstinate finishing, that was the whole point of the pact, and if Thomas Mann forgets this in the finale, this throws – if not a shaft of lightning, then at least a candlelight – on the autobiographical furore in which he let any conception of art slide in order to offer his own self completely.

Doctor Faustus was to be Mann's *Parsifal*, that is how it was planned, and everything after seemed to him just epilogue and pastime. *The Holy Sinner* was still to come, his final masterpiece on the tangle of love, murder and the desire of the flesh, the last novel on the 'indispensable idea' of forgiveness.[157] But even the latest short works stand under the spell of the old theme. *The Black Swan* deals with it in the variant of sickness; a tumour of the sexual organs 'with concomitant haemorrhages' – the adjective in every sense justified – kills off Rosalie after her desire is aroused.[158] The essay 'On Schiller' speaks of the morally destructive idea of shattered faith, the 'necessity to live a lie'; of the monstrosity that it means for the poet of *Demetrius* that at the pinnacle of success he should be tortured by the theme of deceit, the theme of deception and illusion, 'with whose secret a soul parted for ever from the truth must live alone and go forward'.[159]

Finally, the ultimate novel, the second part of the confidence trickster fragment, celebrates once again the slaughter of the sacrificial victim that arouses the flame of desire. Felix Krull, although 'somewhat queasy' and 'not the man for national massacres',[160] is taken to the bullring where there has to be stabbing with bare steel and a thick wave of blood gushing into the sand, unpleasant for him to watch, but making his mistress's bosom surge.[161] Unpleasant to watch, but in no circumstances to avoid: this is the law that right to the end allows no escape. The very last sentence of this last novel pronounces yet again the little words in which everything – artistry, desire, cruelty – seems to join for a final farewell: 'And high and stormy, under my ardent caresses, stormier than at the Iberian game of blood, I saw the surging of that queenly bosom.'[162]

The concluding sentence of a life's work, in which a compulsion seems to keep watch that pleasure cannot surge without the bloody game being joined.

CHAPTER THREE

CREDEMI

WHAT SHALL WE do with all this? The reader might well say that the author should have asked the question before taking two chapters to discuss it. One thing at least is clear: even if a *deus malignus* saw to it that in all doubtful aspects of the diary affair, the apparently less plausible possibility was in fact always the correct one, the problem would still remain to explain why this chain of motifs runs so densely and forcefully through Thomas Mann's entire work. What seems to prevail here is the compulsion to confess, the stubborn and ultimately imploring will to be heard; the muted knocking that someone locked in might give, if he believes himself surrounded by enemies and has to be cautious. And it is impossible to shake off the impression that the guilt which time and again seeks to make itself known is guilt of a non-hypochondriac kind.

What if Mann actually did *mean* what he said? If what has always been taken as metaphor should instead be understood literally?

The secret of his life would then be concealed in similar fashion to Poe's purloined letter, dangled before all eyes yet unseen thanks to this most subtle of all disguises. And if the unthinkable is in fact thought for a moment, does not everything suddenly appear in a new light?

Let us for a moment play Devil's advocate – the Devil that appeared to him in Palestrina. We can venture the thought experiment that if Thomas Mann had committed an actual crime and sought to give an account of it in his work, this work would not have taken a very different form than it actually has. What more could he have done? How many more confessions need he smuggle in, how often should he repeat yet again that everything is strict and undisguised autobiography, that he only ever speaks of himself and has never invented anything?

The converse certainly does not immediately follow. But let us stick for a moment to the assumption that what is confessed in art rests on an actual misdeed. Could this deed then be pinned down: in kind, in place and in time? When and where would it have occurred?

In *Little Herr Friedemann* the rage that flares up is still directed against the 'Mann' himself. The story dates from before the author's second trip to Italy. In *Tobias Mindernickel*, 'T.M.' already has the untellable behind him. The title emerges for the first time in a letter of July 1897.[1] Before this date, therefore, something may have happened that Mann elaborates in this work, in a first phase of coping with it, when he seeks, still rather awkwardly, to remove some traumatic event from his body by writing it down.[2]

The response to the question, therefore, as to the latest date of the event, would be spring 1897. But what would be the earliest date? That is harder to determine, as it is difficult to assess the delay at which literary treatment followed experience. Nonetheless, a dividing line seems to have been Mann's second visit to Naples in November 1896. On 8 November he writes to Grautoff of 'taxing and tiring experiences' on which he had spent a regrettable amount of energy. These experiences, taxing but clearly not traumatic, probably took place in Munich, for they strengthened his inclination to leave Germany and 'make off to the furthest and most alien south . . .' That is precisely where he now finds himself, and he compares the imperial profile of Rome with the charming rabble of Naples, the fine-eyed physiognomy that had attracted his attention for the last four days: 'its sensuous, sweet, southern beauty grabs me ever more.'[3] This sensuous portrait leads on to the poison of sexuality, to the procurers who would not be shaken off and offer him not only young girls, and to the rice diet which he had almost decided upon. The tone of the letter is mixed, but in no way gloomy or guilt-laden.

On his return from Naples, however, the tone changes; not dramatically, but perceptible nonetheless. In his next long report from Rome on 13 January 1897, he describes himself as 'tetchy, sombre and tired'.[4] Two weeks later, he says that he is growing ever more accustomed to 'feeling at home in the dark . . .', which even without the ellipsis would not sound very reassuring.[5] In April he writes of his 'unkempt nerves', which he is trying in every way to strengthen; he drops the phrase of the Augean stable of his conscience.[6] Before June, he is once more in Rome and Naples, as a tour guide for Count Vitzthum.[7] In July he finished

Little Lucy, which he characterized as a strange and ugly tale, 'as befits my present view of the world and its people'.[8]

At the same time, however, he is happy that since *Little Herr Friedemann* he has been freed of 'certain chains'.[9] In April he was already facing his future work with pleasure and confidence, and in the summer he started to draft *Buddenbrooks*. The triumph of art at the very moment when within he was dark and heavy of conscience – is that not reminiscent of the pact with the Devil in which only a sinful act can bring the 'breakthrough'?

It was in the summer of 1897 that Thomas Mann had his encounter with the uninvited guest: a vision that, if you want to be clinical about it, seems a not unusual symptom of post-traumatic stress. In Leverkühn's case the trauma is the contact with the hetaera whom he followed to Hungary when he was twenty-one. Thomas Mann was himself twenty-one when he made his second journey to Naples. The previous year he had visited there briefly in the company of his brother Heinrich. Was he also affected then by the tinge of seduction that drove him to return a second time, free from his brother's supervision?[10] This would be the reason why he later drew on the Nietzsche legend and had Leverkühn, touched by the arm of Esmeralda, first flee but return a year later under the sway of this first contact; and Serenus Zeitblom would speak for his master when he seeks to report this part of the story in as tactful a fashion as possible, tactful also towards himself, 'to whom the telling is like a serious personal confession'.[11]

Leverkühn in any case returns to the place where the naked drive spitefully touched him, and follows the seductress to Hungary. What does Hungary have to do with Italy, or is 'Hungary' only a cipher and password in some homosexual code?[12] On a couple of occasions in *Doctor Faustus* there are discreet connections; Adrian meets Hungarians in the Roman salon that he visits, and the Hungarian noblewoman Frau von Tolna also travels to Naples.[13] The love teacher of Felix Krull, whom he meets in the café where he drinks a glass of punch[14] while others are playing dominoes, is also from Hungary: this being, as the reader of *A Sketch of My Life* and *Doctor Faustus* will recall, both Mann's and Leverkühn's evening occupation during the Roman winter.[15]

Between Hungary and Italy there are evidently secret connections, and the half-way point is Vienna. This is where Rosza ends up on her way through the brothels,[16] and it is likewise where Thomas Mann, at the age of twenty-one, made a stop in June 1896 before travelling on to Italy. Thirty years later he wrote about this short visit, saying that in three days he had managed to fritter away 200 gold marks; 'even though,' he adds – whether in amusement or deliberately cryptically – 'I only stayed at the good old Hotel Klomser on the Herrengasse'.[17] This is also the street where Leverkühn alights after the first performance of his fateful violin concerto, which Mann has take place in Vienna. The concerto is a love token to which Adrian has been persuaded by his pressing friend, the Platonic child that Schwerdtfeger wants from him.[18] From Vienna he travels with his friend, not to Naples, but to Madame de Tolna's Hungarian estate, where Schwerdtfeger's urgency attains its non-Platonic goal. And in this way, in the logic of the novel, the arrow of revenge is already placed on the bowstring.

Leverkühn's act of revenge is highly indirect and mediated; at which point, and after this long extended moment, we can return to speculate as to what the content of the possible deed might have been. We cannot conclude that a crime actually took place simply from the fact that Mann's work would not appear very different if he sought to confess an actual crime. We should not deceive ourselves here; we are adrift in a sea of uncertainties, between the reefs and maws of over- and under-evaluation, with just a few islands of increased plausibility. Such a spot of more or less firm ground is the supposition that the traumatizing act must have been an offence in the realm of desire, and that a mere visit to a prostitute would not have been sufficient to explain the burning guilt and trail of blood. Anything more specific, as in the case of Svidrigalov, has to be left to the more or less willing imagination of the reader.

This speculative imagination, however, is not needed to focus on the most extreme point, which the biographer Donald Prater unknowingly indicates when he notes that *The Wardrobe* ends with a sexual murder.[19] It would be too much to say that Thomas Mann could not hurt a fly; he whipped Bashan, and his depictions of dog chastisement, which take years to grow somewhat calmer, betray how his blood could rise in violent temper.[20] After the Second World War, quite the injured narcissist, he wanted to see a million Germans eradicated.[21] Yet it is simply impossible to think of him venting his wrath in murderous violence. If that strikes the reader as just a lack of imagination on my part, the following cool considerations may suffice. Assume that Thomas Mann had fled Naples with a freshly committed murder on his hands, would he then have returned the following spring, in no matter how troubled a state? Would he have spent a further year in Italy if anything actionable had occurred, would he not rather have made his way home as quickly as possible? Quite apart from the fact that there was no unexplained murder in either Rome or Naples at the time in question: at least none recorded in the archives.[22] Wouldn't the expression 'voluptuousness and hot guilt' also be rather too *weak* a designation for an act of boiling – let alone deadly – violence? And conversely, might not someone who saw himself as a 'lover' because he exchanged a shy kiss also understand by murder something much more trivial?

'Hell is for the pure,'[23] explains the narrator in *Joseph*, and it is quite likely that a crime almost committed, or only indirect participation in a crime, would have sufficed to plunge the life of this sensitive moralist into a guilt feeling that had to be reworked time and again. A moralist such as Thomas Mann might well experience as crime what for a stupid blockhead would be only a misdemeanour. Judah, Leverkühn, the Holy Sinner or the fisherman in that story, feel guilty even though they are so only in a very indirect sense, only 'caught up in the action' as Zeitblom says of Adrian. Christian Buddenbrook is possibly not even caught up, but only a witness – yet perhaps it is sufficient to have been present and not to have intervened, to be swept up in the whirl of events that also seized the dreaming Aschenbach?

Not the least difficulty with this speculation is that we do not know whether we are lumping together things that should actually be kept distinct. The diary speaks of secrets in the plural, not just of one. Perhaps there was a whole series of incidents. There are the thematic chains of dogs, of knives, of pimps, of rape, and also of impotence; there are the supposedly good reasons that the girl in *The Wardrobe* mentions and that indicate an act of defence, of just revenge, or a violent reaction to deep humiliation. In *Doctor Faustus* the action divides into a hot and a cold story: the hot one of the encounter with Esmeralda which sets off the trauma, the cold one of the indirect murder of the lover, for more or less good reasons; in between the story of the guilt at the death of the beloved boy, which even if imagined is experienced as inner reality. It is difficult, if not impossible, to break through the veils and masks to the living kernel. If there was someone to whisper it to us, if a reliable and solid spirit tapped the message on a dinner plate, for instance, that in a Naples park Mann had witnessed a bloody act between hustlers – or in the *mala vita* quarter he followed a young girl, proved impotent and flared up when she made fun of him – or if he fell prey to an attempted rape and took revenge – the evidence would immediately jell together. But in each case the evidence is different, and something is always left over. Or might it be significant that at the turn of the century southern Italy was the centre of European Satanism, as a professor of ethnology informed me after the German edition of the present book was published – the centre of Satanic circles in which homosexual initiation rites as well as animal sacrifice were customary, and which even tourists were taken to see? This would throw an even darker and perhaps impenetrable light on the presumed events, while it might help to explain the chain of ritual animal slaughters as well as the overwhelming, if clandestine, role of the Devil in Mann's oeuvre from the very beginning of *Budden-*

brooks (starting from the exclamation 'Deuce take it!') through to his last short story *The Black Swan* – this bird being traditionally considered a diabolic symbol.[24]

But perhaps everything, like the Devil in Palestrina, is just imagination? This would be the thesis at the other end of the scale: a thesis for which a certain case can be made, even if with some difficulty. It would run more or less as follows. We need no further assumptions, all that is needed is the combination of posing, topos and fantasy. With this triad the riddle can be solved. The holy or unholy face of the criminal – beloved of so many authors of the time! It was precisely the bourgeois scions who liked to see themselves beset with demons – so typical of the turn of the century and its *ecce homo* gestures! Mann was not exactly unique with his child-women, crimes of lust and unspeakable debauches – the most conventional literary topoi of his generation. Where would we end up if every author who likes to let blood flow was accused of personal involvement? The author of *Lulu* would certainly have been threatened with immediate imprisonment. And conversely, is there not an extremely effective guilt that rests solely on the imagination? Proust believed himself to blame for the death of his mother, a feeling that played a great part in the genesis of his work, even if Madame Proust might not have lived a single day longer without her wayward son. A powerful imagination can be sufficient source for an oceanic work. And there is no better example of this than *Doctor Faustus* itself. There evidently were fantasies of revenge and murder that Thomas Mann transposed to Schwerdtfeger from the Ehrenberg episode. Yet while the violinist was shot, Paul

Ehrenberg lived to a ripe old age. The imaginative power of the writer should not be undervalued, his ability to make a mountain out of a molehill; it was not only something real, but also something forcefully imagined, that could cast a shadow covering his life's work.

This is all well and good, but it is not completely convincing. What starts with *Tobias Mindernickel* and is paraded for almost sixty years has nothing to do with a pose. What the still unknown Thomas Mann thought of in Rome was not posing and *ecce homo* gestures, but simply how to convey his experiences to the public – not his dreams or imaginings. The nickname of his last sinful hero was *Credemi*; this could well be inscribed above Mann's entire work. He makes use of literary topoi when they suit him; but he writes always of himself. The first tale of murder bears the signature T.M., and as well as steering all sources discreetly in one direction, he also placed recognizable autobiographical markers at times when abjection was no longer the literary fashion. The theme is not only too obsessive to be a mere stylistic pose, it is often too concealed; a poser does not place himself at a scarcely visible margin.

So could the act to be confessed be merely imaginary? Thomas Mann insisted that he did not invent anything. And, hand on heart, is it credible that a fantasy could traumatize him so severely that he has to turn it round and round for the rest of his life? It is unlikely that the secrets of his life could bear only on the imaginary, and just as unlikely that in the diary affair Thomas Mann should have considered suicide for the sake of such imaginings. 'All actuality is *deadly* earnest',[25] and conversely, the deadly secrets actually happened. The deep and heavy guilt, and the themes of violence and confession that cannot be read away, however much they may also be the work of an exaggerating imagination, cannot owe their origin to this, for what should such imagination crystallize around if not a kernel of experience?

What this kernel precisely was – 'something real with a bloody issue',[26] as Johnny Bishop put it – we do not know. The truth lay in the early diaries and was buried with their ashes. And so we must content ourselves with establishing that a great unknown remains in Mann's biography; a shadow that is cast by a real phantom; a fuzzy spot on an X-ray image.

What would he have become without this unknown? 'One must only need to more than the rest, then one makes oneself a name among men.'[27] Guilt provided the necessary stimulus for Mann's work, but this is not all it did. Without it, Thomas Mann would not have become the great psychologist of world literature that his readers honour. We can go further and not flinch from the apparent paradox: he would not even have become the great humorist. The sense of guilt gives both humour and spiritual insight a depth that is not afforded to the innocent. Without this substratum, his art would remain flat; this is the inner truth of the pact with the Devil.

'It is as well,' so Mann wrote in *Death in Venice*, 'that the world knows only a fine piece of work and not also its origins'; these 'would often confuse readers and shock them, and the excellence of the writing would be of no avail'.[28] But in this case perhaps the outcome is different – perhaps Mann's work actually gains in this way. It has certainly not altered the least part of it. And yet for all that it is no longer quite the same. The lighting changes, and what was invisible suddenly leaps to the eye. Blood streams into the life mask of the man who was serious when he asked, in the words of his beloved Platen, that the world should know him in order to forgive him.

ACKNOWLEDGEMENT

I WOULD LIKE to express my gratitude to the following people for advice and criticism: Perry Anderson, Jan Assmann, Joachim Fest, Fred Flemming, Thomas Hauschild, Eckhard Heftrich, Nikolaus Heidelbach, Hanjo Kesting, Nele and Paul Maar, Christian Milz, Martin Mosebach, Thomas Poiss, Wolfgang Rihm and Hans Wollschläger. My thanks to Wolf Lepenies and the Berliner Wissenschaftskolleg, where the theses of this book were delivered for the first time, for their encouraging reception.

TRANSLATOR'S NOTE

F OLLOWING STANDARD practice, quotations have been inserted from English editions of Thomas Mann's work where these are available. If it has been necessary to modify the translation, this is shown in square brackets in the endnotes, as is any further comment on my part.

The great bulk of English translations of Thomas Mann's fiction and essays were made by Helen Lowe-Porter, who did valiant service in the quantity of her work, and whose rendering of Mann's often elliptical style has been highly praised. It is generally recognized today, however, that her translations are not free of significant errors. Some examples of these are given by David Luke in the introduction to his new translation of *Death in Venice and Other Stories*, London 1998, pp. xlvii ff., though these mostly bear on straightforward points of language. One mistake that David Luke picks up, however, falls into a different category, with particular relevance to the texts of Thomas Mann that Michael Maar discusses. Ms Lowe-Porter has 'almost incredibly' omitted the very last sentence of *Death in Venice*, in which Aschenbach dies believing in a future reunion with Tadzio. In the present book, with its focus on Thomas Mann's homosexuality, boy-love and motif of sexual violence, the fact that several passages that are central to Michael Maar's argument have similarly disappeared in the English editions acquires a keener significance. Typically it is a short phrase, even a word, with which Mann 'betrays' to the careful reader the homosexual character of a depicted event, that has been omitted in this way; the endnotes indicate where I have had to retranslate these passages. And that this was not just an idiosyncrasy of Ms Lowe-Porter is shown by the mistranslation referred to in note 26 to chapter 1, where as recently as 1990 Richard and Clara Winston managed to reverse the meaning of a key letter in which Mann avows his love of boys. At work here is most likely an unconscious desire on the translators' part to convey to English readers a text shorn where possible of unacceptable warts.

As far as concerns the fiction that was translated into English in his lifetime, it would seem that Mann had every confidence in Ms Lowe-Porter, and that her little omissions slipped through unnoticed by the author. A more accurate translation would not have attracted censorship, either in the USA or in Britain. There is one text, however, where the English translation was curtailed by two whole pages – a passage that is important to Michael Maar's argument – and this time with Mann's express consent.[1] This is the celebrated speech on *The German Republic*, in which Mann argues that the homoeroticism that was a salient feature of right-wing terrorist bands could find an alternative outlet in a democratic politics. It is not hard to understand how, in the very different conditions of the Second World War, when Mann was the unchallenged intellectual leader of the German emigration, in an ever-puritanical America, and when a standard trope of anti-Nazi propaganda had been the alleged sexual perversity of Hitler and his followers, this speech from 1922 could appear in English only in this truncated form. It is not just out of historical interest, however, but to make Michael Maar's case more intelligible to English readers, that they should have access to the following passage, which in the 1942 Knopf collection of Mann's political essays, *Order of the Day*, would appear before the section break on page 42.

EXTRACT FROM
THE GERMAN REPUBLIC

I WILL VENTURE in this connection, which remains a
political one, and with all due caution and respect, to speak
of the particular realm of feeling that was alluded to in my
last remarks: that zone of eroticism, in other words, where the
law of sexual polarity that is generally credited proves inopera-
tive, superfluous, and where what we see linked in passionate
communion is like with like, maturer masculinity with admiring
youth, in which this masculinity may idolize a dream of itself, or
young masculinity see a model for itself. Our society, which for
a long while contained this unconsciously, either expelling it
from awareness or prudishly misconstruing it, is gradually beginning to relax the taboo of denial and disrepute imposed on this
phenomenon, to look it more calmly in the face, and to articulate
its many-sidedness in properly human terms. It can indeed signify
enervation, degeneration, sickness, and in such cases it is debat-
able whether the right way to deal with it is discipline or humani-
tarian care. But it is impossible to attribute fundamentally to the
sphere of decay a complex of feeling that can contain what is most
holy and most culturally fertile. Whoever conceives nature and

its laws in the manner of Novalis, who in other words believes these are something to be overcome, will find the reproach of unnaturalness or anti-naturalness a trivial one right from the start; Goethe, moreover, already rejected this common argument with the remark that the phenomenon in question was completely within nature and humanity rather than outside of it, as it had made its appearance at all times and among all peoples, and was to be explained in aesthetic terms by the fact that objectively the masculine is the more pure and fine expression of the human ideal. Schopenhauer put it very similarly . . .

The aspect of this remarkable subject that I want to bring to attention here is the political one, something that is also not lacking. Is it not said that the War, with its experiences of comradeship in blood and death, the harsh and exclusive masculinity of its way of life and atmosphere, has powerfully strengthened this erotic realm? The political attitude of its believers is generally nationalistic and militarist, and it is said that relationships of this kind form the secret cement of the monarchist leagues, indeed, that an erotic-political emotion after the model of certain loving friendships of antiquity lies at the root of particular terrorist acts of our days. But Harmodios and Aristogeiton were democrats; and it cannot be said that what seems the rule today is based on any more fundamental law. The most powerful modern counter-example is the poet of the Calamus songs, Walt Whitman,

Resolv'd to sing no songs to-day but those of manly attachment,
Projecting them along that substantial life,
Bequeathing hence types of athletic love.

With these songs, this bodily-athletic love, Whitman sought to 'make the continent indissoluble', to 'create divine magnetic lands', 'inseparable cities with their arms about each other's necks, / By the love of comrades, / By the manly love of comrades'. Eros as statesman, even as the creator of states, is a trusted old idea, which in our day has been intellectually propagated anew; but it is basically nonsense to seek to make its cause and party expression a monarchist restoration. Its cause is rather the republic, in other words the unity of state and culture to which we give this name, and even if no pacifist in the vegetarian sense, it is by its very nature a god of peace, which between states as well seeks to establish 'without edifices or rules or trustees or any argument, / The institution of the dear love of comrades'.

I did not want to leave unremarked, or ignore in my attempt to convince you, a sphere of sensibility that without a doubt contains within it, or can contain, elements important to state and culture. Health? Sickness? Be careful with these notions, they are the most difficult in all of philosophy and ethics! Whitman's worship of boys, since in his case it forms but one fine province of the all-embracing realm of his phallically healthy, phallically brimming inspiration, was certainly something more healthy than poor Novalis with his love for the pale Sophia, Novalis who found it wise to love a sleeping form in order to prepare a convivial resting-place 'for the night', and in whose erotic Holy Communion the stimulable lecherousness of the consumptive uncannily breaks through.

NOTES

NOTES TO CHAPTER ONE

1 On 17 March 1933, writing from Lenzerheide, Thomas Mann arranged for Golo to be summoned to Munich. For a moment, at least, this calmed his fears, and when Golo arrived in Munich two days later, he noted: 'I am now somewhat relieved about my old diaries and papers, which characteristically were my first and main concern.' This relief however did not last very long. On 1 April he consoled himself that he had begun to grow accustomed to the fact that he would not be able to return to his customary life in the foreseeable future. The thought that immediately followed was: 'I am much concerned about having my papers sent here, old diaries etc.' (Thomas Mann, *Diaries 1918–1939*, ed. Hermann Kesten, trans. Richard and Clara Winston, London 1984, p. 142). A week later, in Lugano, the news was worse: 'One must be prepared for house searches. Fresh anxiety about my old diaries. Imperative to bring them to safety' (7 April 1933; *Diaries 1918–1939*, p. 147). The following day he sent Golo a letter and the key.

2 Golo Mann, *Reminiscences and Reflections: Growing Up in Germany*, trans. Krishna Winston, London 1990, p. 302.

3 Both Erika Mann and Peter de Mendelssohn still assumed that Hans

Holzner took the case right away to the Munich 'Brown House', instead of to the station. (Cf. *Tagebücher 1933–34*, p. xi.) In point of fact, Holzner did take the case to the station, but on instructions from Munich it was searched by the frontier police at Lindau. They, however, were interested only in publishing contracts and other documents with a bearing on tax matters; the diaries were taken for drafts of novels and therefore considered irrelevant. Cf. Jürgen Kolbe, *Heller Zauber. Thomas Mann in München 1894–1933*, Berlin 1987, pp. 414 ff.

4 Golo Mann, *Reminiscences and Reflections*, pp. 302 ff.

5 [Extracts from Thomas Mann's diaries, unless given from the much abbreviated English edition, are cited simply by date of entry. They may be consulted in the ten-volume *Tagebücher* edited by Peter de Mendelssohn and Inge Jens, Frankfurt 1979–95.]

6 'That this actually was everything, the entire diaries up to 1933, we did not suspect and learned only from the packets left after his death' (Erika Mann, 'Das letzte Jahr. Bericht über meinen Vater', *Autobiographisches*, Frankfurt 1968, p. 7). In fact the burning took place in stages. The first auto-da-fé was in 1896. On 21 June 1944 Thomas Mann remarked on the 'destruction of old diaries'. The following year he burnt still more of his diaries in his garden incinerator at Pacific Palisades, observed by Golo (cf. *Tagebücher 1933–34*, pp. xii ff.). On 15 September 1950 he had it in mind again to burn all his old diaries, but instead sealed them for a period of twenty-five years, later reduced to twenty. From the entry for 13 October 1950 it is clear that his intention was for these diaries to be made available for research after his death. From March 1933 to August 1955 they are complete, but the only earlier volume that has remained unscathed, as he used it as a source for *Doctor Faustus*, comprises the years 1918–21.

7 Erika Mann, *Autobiographisches*, pp. 7 ff.

8 *Diaries 1918–1939*, p. 154 [translation modified].

9 In grammatical terms, the two contrasting principles are 'constancy of subject' versus 'positional contact'. If there is a literary form in which the latter comes into its own, then it is undoubtedly that of the diary. Quite apart from this, however, there is something demonic in the way that precisely the important passages seem forcibly compressed into ambiguity – though perhaps these only show how hard it always is to understand someone correctly. Such understanding, however, is the object of the following considerations.

10 Golo Mann, *Reminiscences and Reflections*, p. 302.

11 At the start of his exile Thomas Mann fell prey to severe attacks of depression. To give just two examples from the beginning and the end of that gloomy year: 'Horrible sense of frenzy, helplessness, twitching muscles, almost a shivering fit, and feared losing my rational faculties' (18 March 1933; *Diaries 1918–1939*, p. 130); and 'Tormenting, deep depression and hopeless conditions, hard to bear, a kind of mental goose-flesh, repeated time and again after brighter spells' (4 November 1933).

12 Two diary entries in 1920 are especially significant on his feelings towards the 14-year-old Klaus. On 25 July he writes: 'Am enraptured with Eissi, terribly handsome in his swimming trunks. Find it quite natural that I should fall in love with my son' (*Diaries 1918–1939*, p. 101). And on 17 October, 'I heard some noise in the boys' room and came upon Eissi totally nude and up to some nonsense by Golo's bed. Deeply struck by his radiant adolescent body; overwhelming.' This is followed by one of those typical editorial ellipses; a protective decency which the potential diary browser would certainly not have appreciated.

13 We do not know whether the diaries from this early time were still

extant at this point. Golo Mann speaks only of the notes from the 1920s; cf. *Reminiscences and Reflections*, p. 303; the 'oilcloth-covered notebooks' that fitted with other material into a suitcase may have included the thirty or so volumes used to cover the entire century to date (to take the average from the years 1918–21, precisely four years in four volumes). In later notes Thomas Mann may have looked back at the earlier ones, so that there would be no great difference as far as incriminating material was concerned.

14 To use Mann's own expression, 'As for myself there is no doubt that "even" the *Betrachtungen (Reflections of a Nonpolitical Man)* are an expression of my sexual inversion' (17 September 1919; *Diaries 1918–1939*, p. 66).

15 An earlier and a more recent example. Jürgen Kolbe in 1987 wrote in somewhat hedged fashion: 'No one should be able to exploit TM's secrets and rush to the market with the muted needs and joys of his "lunar syntax". In the hands of the Nazis these notes would have been a deadly weapon' (*Heller Zauber*, p. 414). Martin Meyer, twelve years later, still writes in similar vein: 'What there would have been could probably be concluded from additional assumptions in respect to those sporadic indications that Thomas Mann scattered from time to time in his diary for the rest of his life: on the one hand politics, the back and forth of conflicting feelings towards the "movement" under way in Germany since the 1920s. And on the other hand the homoerotic drive – which probably did not underlie the self-censorship of the chronicler after 1933, for the simple reason that there were no actual adventures to report: from this time on shy, occasionally more direct, glances at the unattainable had to suffice; or else a nostalgia, triggered by memories, for what the suitcase would have conveyed in terms of experience' (*Tagebuch und spätes Leid. Über Thomas Mann*, Munich/Vienna 1999,

pp. 20 ff.). But the possibility that political vacillations might have been the basis for Mann's fears is undermined by Meyer himself: 'In any case it would not have needed too keen an imagination to "reconstruct" the mental orientation of these diaries: it emerges clear as day, after all, in the *Reflections of a Nonpolitical Man*, what the author was then committed to – or better, what he was committed against' (ibid., p. 101). This is precisely it: everything was already there in the *Reflections*. And even if Thomas Mann had been unable to escape a reluctant fascination for the sturdy SA columns with their openly male-bonding character, the open display of such vacillations, however unpleasant it might have been for him, would scarcely have been sufficient reason for him seriously to consider suicide. In his tough and unconditional will to grow old so as to leave behind him a late work, Thomas Mann was indistinguishable from Gustav von Aschenbach. Above all, vacillations of this kind could not be denoted by the expression 'secrets of my life'.

16 30 April 1933. *Diaries 1918–1939*, p. 154.

17 *Notizbücher 7–14*, ed. Hans Wysling and Yvonne Schmidlin, Frankfurt 1992, p. 112.

18 Hermann Kurzke, *Thomas Mann. Das Leben als Kunstwerk*, Munich 1999, p. 517. Cf. also Klaus Harpprecht: 'Had he, for all his high-minded and strict principles, let himself purchase some pretty young boy – in Venice, or perhaps Naples? This may well have been.' *Thomas Mann. Eine Biographie*, Reinbek bei Hamburg 1995, p. 91.

19 Thomas Mann, *Briefe an Otto Grautoff 1894–1901 und Ida Boy-Ed 1903–1928*, ed. Peter de Mendelssohn, Frankfurt 1975, p. 81.

20 Cf. the important study by Karl Werner Böhm, *Zwischen Selbstzucht und Verlangen. Thomas Mann und das Stigma Homosexualität*, Würzburg 1991, p. 381 and passim.

21 *Briefe an Otto Grautoff*, p. 30.

22 *Tonio Kröger*, in *Death in Venice and other stories*, trans. David Luke, London 1998, p. 139.

23 This is why Heinrich Detering's study on poetic camouflage, *Das offene Geheimnis. Zur literarischen Produktivität eines Tabus von Winckelmann bis zu Thomas Mann*, Göttingen 1994, no longer takes *Death in Venice* into account: it is clearly beyond the limit where camouflage ceases.

24 This is what Mann himself said with regard to Richard Wagner, speaking in poetic drama through the mouth of Siegmund. (Thomas Mann, *Gesammelte Werke*, ed. Peter de Mendelssohn, Frankfurt 1960–74, vol. IX, p. 409.)

25 Weber was a teacher at the Wickersdorf free school, a poet and avowed homosexual. Cf. Hans Wisskirchen, 'Republikanischer Eros. Zu Walt Whitmans und Hans Blühers Rolle in der politischen Publizistik Thomas Manns', in *'Heimsuchung und süßes Gift.' Erotik und Poetik bei Thomas Mann*, ed. Gerhard Härle, Frankfurt 1992, p. 24.

26 *Letters of Thomas Mann 1889–1955*, trans. Richard and Clara Winston, Berkeley and Los Angeles, CA, 1990, p. 93. [This translation has been modified: the Winstons render Mann's '*kaum bedingt*' as 'scarcely' instead of 'scarcely qualified', thus reversing the author's meaning, which he makes still more clear in the letter referred to in note 27. The original can be found in *Briefe*, vol. I: *1889–1936*, ed. Erika Mann, Frankfurt 1979, pp. 176 ff.]

27 *Letters of Thomas Mann*, p. 96.

28 *Die Briefe Thomas Manns. Regesten und Register*, vol. I, Frankfurt 1987, p. 293 (20/72).

29 Thomas Mann, 'Über die Ehe', *Gesammelte Werke* VIII, pp. 195–9.

30 *Gesammelte Werke* XI, pp. 847 and 849. Cf. in particular Wisskirchen,

'Republikanischer Eros', pp. 17–40. [An English translation of Mann's speech *The German Republic* is given in *Order of the Day*, trans. H. T. Lowe-Porter, New York 1942. This however has been purged of a two-page passage referred to here that discusses homosexuality and politics, see 'Extract from *The German Republic*', pp. 113–15.]

31 Wisskirchen, 'Republikanischer Eros', pp. 27–31. The events that Thomas Mann reflected in his speech were the assassinations of Erzberger in 1921 and Rathenau the following year, murders that were planned and carried out by monarchist secret societies. Wisskirchen assumes that the Municher Thomas Mann had additional information on the homosexual character of these male bands.

32 Thus Hans Mayer's commentary on Mann's liaison with Klaus Heuser. Cf. *Heller Zauber*, p. 15.

33 Homosexual circles within the Nazi movement initially had high hopes of liberalization, which were all the more bitterly disappointed with the murder of Röhm. Cf. Hans Blüher, 'Die Gründung des 3. Reiches', afterword to Pierre Klossowski, *Die aufgehobene Berufung*, Munich 1997. The other side of this coin is that in April 1933, when he still had to be assured of the SA's allegiance, Hitler could not have ordered a major campaign against homosexuals.

34 Such glances are found regularly in the diaries. Before the journey from Sanary to Zurich, Thomas Mann packed 'boxes and several cases, including my black suitcase with the diaries and papers, which had caused me such worry' (23 January 1934).

35 A word Mann disavows in his letter to Kurt Martens of 28 March 1906, responding to Martens's characterizing him as an 'ascetic' (*Letters of Thomas Mann*, p. 50).

36 Gerhard Härle sees in Mann's work 'an archaic consciousness of guilt and deviation' ('Simulationen der Wahrheit', in *'Heimsuchung*

und süßes Gift', p. 75). In the preface to this volume of essays, Härle explains that 'in the writer's universe of values, erotic desire does not just signify increased pleasure and adventure, but forms the origin of a consciousness of guilt' – a 'guilt that is never completely depressing, but also never completely atoned', and proves to be the stimulus for the entire work (ibid., p. 8). The notion of stimulating guilt is certainly of key importance, but that homoeroticism was 'the fixed point of Mann's productive guilt consciousness' (p. 9) we shall dispute below. This interpretation has its reasons, it is even plausible, but not completely so. It leaves unilluminated a little decisive something, like a moon that rises time and again, but never reaches fullness.

37 *Death in Venice*, in *Death in Venice and other stories*, p. 244. This is how Mann saw it even in his youth. To the self-accusation of Grautoff, who sought to be cured of his homosexuality by hypnosis and visited the celebrated doctor Albert Moll, he answers that this ugly whining got on his nerves and raised his 'simple and stubborn pride, which knows that the whole world is innocent and stands seven times innocent before necessity'. Why should he suddenly view Grautoff through the eyes of a country vicar? 'You are for me someone who understands unhappiness very well, with an insight into a good part of the mystical, sad and interesting vileness of God's creation – but beyond this nothing. The instinct you believe should lead me to feel "repugnance and loathing" towards you is completely foreign to me [. . .] *You are innocent!'* (letter of 6 April 1897, in *Briefe an Grautoff*, pp. 88 ff.).

38 'Über die Ehe', p. 196. [The 'Venetian sonnets' referred to here are those of August von Platen.]

39 'What am I suffering from? From sexuality . . . Is it then going to destroy me? [. . .] How I hate it, this sexuality, which takes every-

thing beautiful as its result and effect! Ah, it is the poison that lurks in all beauty!' (*Briefe an Grautoff*, p. 80).

40 *Diaries 1918–1939*, p. 198.

41 6 May 1934, ibid., p. 210.

42 Letter to Klaus and Erika Mann of 19 October 1927; Erika Mann, *Briefe und Antworten*, vol. I, *1922–1950*, ed. Anna Zanco Prestel, Munich 1984, pp. 17 ff. Mann plays ironically with the meaning of *sündigen*, as he does in his well-known letter of apology to Gerhart Hauptmann (*Briefe* I, p. 234). As far as Klaus Heuser is concerned, nothing would change in the openness with which the family joked about him. On the subject of his remaining unmarried, Erika jibed in 1954: 'Since he could not have the M[agician], he preferred to leave the whole thing well alone' (29 August 1954). 'How relaxed the tone has become!' as Hermann Kurzke remarked quite correctly (*Das Leben als Kunstwerk*, p. 384), but Mann could already be relaxed a full quarter-century earlier.

43 'His remarks on Adrian's character. Anachronism of the student jargon. The homosexual substratum, for the most part intangible' (3 January 1946).

44 '*Bitte sehr!*' in the original. From a letter to Kuno Fiedler of 22 November 1954 (printed in the appendix to *Tagebücher 1953–1955*, ed. Inge Jens, Frankfurt 1995, p. 697). Seven years previously Mann had already severely corrected Fiedler, when he wrote an ill-humoured review of *Doctor Faustus* and saw himself depicted in Zeitblom. (*Thomas Mann. Selbstkommentare: 'Doktor Faustus' und 'Die Entstehung des Doktor Faustus'*, ed. Hans Wysling with the collaboration of Marianne Eich-Fischer, Frankfurt 1992, pp. 196 ff.) The trust shown in this late letter is that much more remarkable.

45 Michael Mann, *Schuld und Segen im Werk Thomas Manns*, celebratory lecture given in Lübeck, 6 June 1975.

46 'Meine Zeit', in Thomas Mann, *Essays*, vol. VI, ed. Hermann Kurzke and Stephan Stachorski, Frankfurt 1977, p. 160.

47 Letter of 12 December 1838; acknowledgement to Henning Ritter for this reference.

48 *Gesammelte Werke* XI, p. 514.

49 Reinhard Baumgart, 'Der erotische Schriftsteller', in *Thomas Mann und München*, Frankfurt 1989, p. 20.

50 Hans Wollschläger, *Wiedersehen mit Dr. F. Beim Lesen in Letzter Zeit*, Göttingen 1997, p. 22.

51 'Sleep, Sweet Sleep', in *Past Masters*, trans. H. T. Lowe-Porter, London 1933, p. 274.

52 *Briefe an Grautoff*, p. 90.

53 Ibid., pp. 106 ff. The verses are part of the refrain from Platen Mann considered as a motto for *Buddenbrooks*. The 'dread' he returns to in his own poem 'Nur eins': 'We, to whom God gave gloomy sense / And pointed out all depths of shame and dread' (ibid., p. 109).

54 Letter to Heinrich Mann of 13 February 1901, *Letters of Heinrich and Thomas Mann 1900–1949*, trans. Don Reneau *et al.*, Berkeley, CA, 1998, p. 46.

55 'A Brother', in *Order of the Day*, p. 156.

56 Letter to Heinrich Mann of 8 January 1904, *Letters of Heinrich and Thomas Mann*, p. 63. Even here the ambiguity is not completely removed, as theoretically at least this could also be read as his having something worse to forget that was done to him. But the far more likely sense is the opposite.

57 'Im Spiegel', in *Gesammelte Werke* XI, pp. 331 ff.

58 Letter of 15 July 1906 to Samuel Fischer; *Thomas Mann. Briefe* vol. III, *1948–1955*, ed. Erika Mann, Frankfurt 1979, p. 451.

59 Thomas Mann, 'Dostoyevsky – in Moderation', preface to *The Short Novels of Dostoyevsky*, New York 1945, p. x.

60 Cf. *Briefe* I, p. 45. In *The Genesis of a Novel*, London 1961, Mann speaks of artistic inhumanity and the 'colouring of existence by this sense of guilt' (p. 144).

61 Cf. Michael Maar, *Geister und Kunst*, Frankfurt 1997, pp. 200 ff. and passim, also Martin Meyer: 'He took it for granted that Katia would completely enter and share his destiny. But along the way Erika was also assigned a kind of sacrificial role – which Mann saw as to her own advantage. This has to be expressed in a harsh fashion, for Mann does so himself. One of the most terrifying sentences in the diary, and at the same time one of his last notes in California, reflects what was simply declared as a 'concern': '[. . .] K[atia]'s suffering on account of E[rika]. My gratitude for her and my concern for her, as she could so easily follow her brother.' And then in the unconcealed expression of a death wish, this sentence: 'Certainly she does not want to live any longer than us' (*Tagebuch und spätes Leid*, p. 79).

62 'Dostoyevsky – in Moderation', p. x.

63 Letter to Ida Boy-Ed of 19 August 1904, cf. *Briefe an Grautoff*, pp. 149 ff. The same year he wrote to his brother Heinrich: '*Der Tag* carried a quite long essay of mine, supposedly on Gabriele Reuter, but taken very generally and personally' (*Letters of Heinrich and Thomas Mann*, p. 48). This 'supposedly on' stands invisibly in the titles of all his essays.

64 'Bilse und ich', in *Gesammelte Werke* X, p. 22.

65 Cf. 'Dostoyevsky – in Moderation', p. xi.

66 Mann wrote to the publisher Paul Steegemann on 18 August 1920: 'Great moralists have mostly been great sinners also. Dostoevsky is said to have been a debaucher of children' (*Letters of Thomas Mann*, p. 98).

67 Sigmund Freud, in his essay on 'Dostoevsky and Parricide', asks

'why there is any temptation to reckon Dostoevsky among the criminals. The answer is that it comes from his choice of material, which singles out from all others violent, murderous and egoistic characters, thus pointing to the existence of similar tendencies within himself, and also from certain facts in his life like his passion for gambling and his possible confession to a sexual assault upon a young girl' (*Standard Edition*, vol. XXI, London 1961, p. 178). The footnote that Freud adds at this point refers among other sources to Stefan Zweig's 1920 publication *Three Masters* (English edition, London 1938), where the question is discussed as to how far Dostoevsky transgressed the bounds of law, and 'how much of the criminal instincts of his heroes was realized in himself'. Mann could also have read in this text about the sado-masochism that Freud imputes to Dostoevsky, and the sexual-neurotic origin of epilepsy and latent homosexuality. Cf. also the commentary to Mann's preface in *Essays VI*.

68 In theory there is no route from one to the other, from the here of life to the there of literature. Even if he seeks to do so in auto-biography, there is no way that the author can bridge this gulf and transpose himself from the disordered here into the planned and prescribed there. The 'I' of the author, whether he will or no, has always a different status from that of a fictional character. What emerges in writing as the 'I' is the *autre moi*, which Marcel Proust sharply distinguishes from the empirical author, with all his vices and vanities, whom Sainte-Beuve wrongly believed he needed only to have dined with enough times in order to form a picture of his creation.

One possible conclusion would be to forbid in principle the drawing of any conclusions back from fiction to lived experience. Yet the price of this ban would be quite serious. It contradicts not only every reader's experience, all intuition, and the common sense that the theorists who propose it hold at bay with the same effort with which they reject its infringement as biographism. Such a general ban also conceals a mountain of interesting little distinctions. And this still does not alter the fact that there are cases in which authors employ different tricks to try and bridge the gulf. It is not Sainte-Beuvism if one refuses to ignore such attempts. On the contrary, it would be philologically dubious to artificially blind oneself to the signals with which an author seeks to entice the reader from the there of fiction into the here of life; an author who in speaking of himself will again not hesitate, if things get too close, to push it all back over the gap into the realm of fiction.

69 Diary entry for 27 April 1951. Perhaps the intention here was a kind of political satire, the fabricated confession of a fellow-traveller in the style of a Soviet forced confession, rather than notes from underground; but nothing more certain can be said on this matter.

70 *Gesammelte Werke* XIII, p. 55: 'I will say that Tolstoy's work is at least as markedly autobiographical as my own tiny effort' (*Briefe* I, p. 62). It is interesting that in discussing the diaries, Martin Meyer quotes four times Mann's apparent claim that 'everything after the *Tonio Kröger* story has essentially nothing to do with his own experience' (*Tagebuch und spätes Leid*, p. 17). Does this mean that Mann lied throughout his whole diary? But if you read on, you can see that Mann says the very opposite. The sentence falls in a passage on the cluelessness of Agnes B. Meyer, Mann's unloved American patron, who was planning a book on him at that time and whom he took as a model for the 'Thamar' episode in *Joseph*. 'Lunch with her. Awkwardnesses treated with incomprehension. The story: great impression. Psychologisms about me for her book. Cluelessness

such as my total lack of involvement with people, the lack of influence of emotion on my writing, at least since Tonio Kröger' (4 June 1942).

NOTES TO CHAPTER TWO

1 *Joseph and His Brothers*, trans. H. T. Lowe-Porter, London 1989, pp. 718–19.

2 *Briefe an Grautoff*, p. 90.

3 On the notion and technique of literary camouflage, cf. Detering, *Das offene Geheimnis*.

4 Cf. Maar, *Geister und Kunst*, pp. 322 ff. What must one not know about Rumpelstiltskin, what is his unmistakable mark of identity? And what does it mean if Goethe in *Der West-Östliche Divan* follows *Morgenröte* with the non-rhyming *Hatem*, if Kafka's protagonist is named 'K.' and Herman Hesse's 'Harry Haller', if on one occasion Proust calls his hero 'Marcel' and Paul Thomas Mann's hero is 'Paolo Hofmann'? Quite certainly in each case it means something different, but in every case a piece of information is missed if one sticks rigidly to one side of the gulf. In Mann's work in particular, the play on his name is revealed time and again as a trick to overcome this gulf, as a camouflage signal and a token that the reference here is to his own empirical and unmistakable Thomas Mann self. Composers from Bach to Shostakovitch have done likewise.

5 *Little Herr Friedemann*, in *Death in Venice and other stories*, pp. 14, 15, 20.

6 Ibid., p. 27.

7 The accumulation of scenes in which a bystander is humiliated – Dedner calls them 'mocking scenes' – has not been unnoticed by Thomas Mann scholars. Cf. Burghard Dedner, 'Entwürdigung. Die

Angst vor dem Gelächter in Thomas Manns Werk', in Härle (ed.), *Heimsuchung und süßes Gift*, pp. 87–102.

8 Cf. Hans Rudolf Vaget, *Thomas Mann. Kommentar zu sämtlichen Erzählungen*, Munich 1984, p. 71. The author of this review, which hovers between alienation and admiration, was Heinrich Mann's friend Ludwig Ewers, Tommy's 'famous enemy' (cf. *Briefe an Grautoff*, p. 90), who considered himself a 'Uranian', as emerges from a letter of Heinrich, and who seems to have been well-informed as to the adolescent needs of Thomas Mann. Heinrich wrote to Ewers that in Tomy's [sic] case sleeping with a not too voracious young girl would suffice to cure everything. Cf. Harpprecht, *Thomas Mann*, pp. 95 ff.

9 On the subtext of this sale scene, cf. Detering, *Das offene Geheimnis*, pp. 163–5.

10 *Tobias Mindernickel*, in *Stories of a Lifetime*, vol. I, trans. H. T. Lowe-Porter, London 1961, p. 63.

11 Ibid., p. 64.

12 Ibid., p. 67.

13 Cf. 'Dostoyevsky – in Moderation', p. viii.

14 *Tobias Mindernickel*, p. 51.

15 Ibid., p. 57.

16 'Über den Alkohol', *Gesammelte Werke* XI, p. 718.

17 *The Wardrobe*, in *Stories of Three Decades*, trans. H. T. Lowe-Porter, p. 77 [translation modified]. Reinhard Baumgart comments on this conclusion: 'A paragraph as sweet in tone as gloomy in deed, glaring in its significance and completely underhand. For who, woman or man, is being stabbed here, and for what "good reason"? And does the emphasis of the attack being fairly "above the waist" not indicate silently that it was rather the zone below that attracted the knife? At any event the good and bad reasons are left unspoken, as

if they were self-explanatory.' (*Selbstvergessenheit. Drei Wege zum Werk: Thomas Mann, Franz Kafka, Bertolt Brecht*, Frankfurt 1993, p. 50.) The good reason is not made any more explicit in Andersen's *The Sandhills of Jutland*, which was one of Mann's possible sources for *The Wardrobe*. Cf. Maar, *Geister und Kunst*, pp. 50 ff.

18 Afterword to *Frühe Erzählungen*, ed. Peter de Mendelssohn, Frankfurt 1981, p. 670. It is not only in Mann's planned stories that knives recur, they do likewise in the world of his dreams. In his seventh notebook, the young fiancé notes down a 'morning dream of Katia': 'When I asked for my medication, the word "jealousy" somehow fell between us, and I said: "Let them be jealous! The more jealous they are, the better!" Then she took a kitchen knife from the table and threatened me with it, apparently in all seriousness.' (*Notizbücher 7–14*, p. 103. The dream dates from 1904.)

19 Cf. Hans Wysling in the *Thomas-Mann-Handbuch*, ed. Helmut Koopmann, Stuttgart 1990, pp. 368 ff.

20 *Buddenbrooks: The Decline of a Family*, trans. H. T. Lowe-Porter, Harmondsworth 1957, p. 446.

21 In his old age, Thomas Mann related this afternoon event in Palestrina, in which he saw the Devil in person sitting on a sofa – a vision he experienced as outrageously oppressive – to the set designer, poet and painter Fabius von Gugel, when the latter was about to make a prolonged visit to Rome. It was from him that the story was handed down to posterity by Peter de Mendelssohn. Cf. *Der Zauberer. Das Leben des deutschen Schriftstellers Thomas Mann. Erster Teil 1875–1918*, Frankfurt 1975, pp. 292 ff. Why Mann should have recognized the visitor right away as the Devil is a question which clearly was never asked. One possibility could be that he was somehow ready and waiting for such a visit. See also chapter 3, p. 100.

22 *Buddenbrooks*, p. 208.

23 Ibid., p. 95.

24 *Tonio Kröger*, p. 191.

25 Cf. *Geister und Kunst*, pp. 108–16.

26 Cf. *Regesten und Register*, p. 49 (03/3).

27 *Tonio Kröger*, pp. 176, 177 [translation modified].

28 Ibid., p. 161.

29 This 'lush ripening' of his art was also what Thomas Mann promised himself when he wrote to Grautoff before his southern journey that he would not be an artist worth the name if he did not 'conceive at least a dozen stories in Italy' (*Briefe an Grautoff*, p. 59). The 'heredity on his mother's side' that drew him there is one of the many autobiographical signals in this story: Thomas Mann's mother Julia Bruhn, born in Brazil, had 'inclinations to the "south", to art, even to Bohemianism', inclinations that her son believed, in the Goethean style, he had inherited from her along with her musicality and her pleasure in spinning yarns. (Cf. *Thomas Mann – Agnes B. Meyer. Briefwechsel 1937–1955*, ed. Hans Rudolf Vaget, Frankfurt 1992, pp. 162 ff.)

30 *Tonio Kröger*, p. 154 [translation modified].

31 This is how Kurzke sees it, in commenting on this passage: 'But this is simply something that Mann dreamed up. The letters to his friend convey no trace of it' (*Das Leben als Kunstwerk*, p. 76). Apart from the fact that it is not quite true, since some traces are actually conveyed, does Kurzke expect Mann to have told his most intimate secrets in a letter? Kurzke misses the literary realization of this descent and concludes that on this occasion at least Mann need not be taken at his word. The present chapter may serve as a commentary on this conclusion.

32 *The Fight Between Jappe and Do Escobar*, in *Stories of Three Decades*, pp. 328–9.

33 Ibid., p. 338.

34 Ibid., p. 331.

35 The subject of the tale is drawn from Mann's notes for *Maja*, the novel of Munich society that he planned after *Buddenbrooks* but never carried out; he also made use of it for *Doctor Faustus*.

36 *Anekdote*, in *Gesammelte Werke* VIII, p. 414.

37 Ibid., p. 415.

38 *Confessions of Felix Krull, Confidence Man: The Early Years*, trans. Denver Lindley, London 1955, p. 124.

39 Ibid., p. 121.

40 Ibid., p. 126.

41 *A Sketch of My Life*, Paris 1930, p. 39.

42 Ibid., p. 41.

43 *The Hungry*, in *Stories of Three Decades*, pp. 170–1.

44 *Death in Venice*, in *Death in Venice and other stories*, p. 252.

45 Ibid., p. 252 [translation modified].

46 Ibid., p. 258.

47 *Tonio Kröger*, p. 154.

48 *Death in Venice*, p. 249.

49 *Gesammelte Werke* X, pp. 698–9.

50 Bruno Frank, *Politische Novelle*, Berlin 1928, pp. 147–80.

51 *Death in Venice*, p. 259.

52 Ibid., p. 246.

53 Ibid., p. 260.

54 Ibid., pp. 260–1.

55 Ibid., p. 261.

56 Thomas Mann, *Aufsätze, Reden, Essays. Band II. 1914–1918*, ed. Harry Matter, Berlin/Weimar 1983, pp. 12, 14. In the *Gesammelte Werke*, the emphasis on this 'testimony of blood' is omitted; Matter takes it from the original edition.

57 *The German Republic*, p. 9.

58 'The Making of *The Magic Mountain*', in *The Magic Mountain*, trans. H. T. Lowe-Porter, London 1999, p. 722.

59 Cf. *Thomas Mann an Ernst Bertram, Briefe aus den Jahren 1910–1955*, ed. Inge Jens, Pfullingen 1960, p. 156.

60 *The Magic Mountain*, p. 491.

61 Ibid., p. 493.

62 Ibid., p. 494.

63 Ibid., p. 496.

64 Ibid., pp. 496–7.

65 Ibid., pp. 124–5.

66 Cf. *Geister und Kunst*, p. 322.

67 *The Magic Mountain*, p. 616.

68 Ibid., p. 462.

69 *Gesammelte Werke* X, p. 880.

70 Ibid., p. 881.

71 Cf. Freud, *Moses and Monotheism* (*Standard Edition* vol. XXIII, p. 135).

72 'Tables of the Law', in *Stories of a Lifetime*, vol. II, London 1961, p. 289.

73 *Mario and the Magician*, in *Stories of a Lifetime*, p. 211.

74 Ibid., p. 212.

75 Apart from Erika's stimulus, with this pistol shot Thomas Mann harks back – or forward – to the story of the tramcar murder, which he intended to tell in *Maja*, and which is central to the plot of *Faustus*.

76 *Briefe I*, pp. 299 ff.

77 *The Transposed Heads*, trans. H. T. Lowe-Porter, London 1941, p. 62.

78 Ibid., pp. 62, 68.

79 *Lotte in Weimar*, trans. H. T. Lowe-Porter, London 1940, p. 272. [In North America this novel is published as *The Beloved Returns*.]

80 Ibid., p. 244.

81 Ibid., p. 220.

82 Ibid., p. 229.

83 Ibid., p. 246.

84 Ibid., p. 248.

85 Ibid., p. 341.

86 How Thomas Mann underlays this with (or perhaps superimposes on it) the literary background of the robber-girl in Hans Christian Andersen's 'The Snow Queen' is explored in *Geister und Kunst*, pp. 174 ff. See also there the similarities made between Rosza and Leverkühn's Hetaera Esmeralda.

87 *Joseph and His Brothers*, p. 117.

88 Ibid., p. 119.

89 Ibid., p. 1004.

90 Ibid., p. 113.

91 Ibid., p. 373.

92 Ibid., p. 374. [Here the translation has been modified, as the key phrase '*in Ängsten der Jungfräulichkeit*' disappears without trace in Ms Lowe-Porter's version.]

93 Ibid., p. 390.

94 'But since we were filled with longing to know each another completely, we set to work at once, and I stayed with her until the following morning.' *Confessions of Felix Krull*, p. 125.

95 *Joseph and His Brothers*, p. 751.

96 Ibid., p. 380.

97 In the carriage, before they set to work, they have an evidently obscene conversation, 'which I scruple to set down, since I am sensible enough to see that its freedom lies beyond the compass of my voluble and chatty pen.' *Confessions of Felix Krull*, p. 123.

98 *Joseph and His Brothers*, p. 377.

 99 Ibid., p. 385.

100 Ibid., p. 410.

101 Ibid., p. 420.

102 Ibid., p. 796.

103 For example, the crocodile that eats its way up the chained prisoner's thigh.

104 *Joseph and His Brothers*, p. 803.

105 Ibid., pp. 813–14.

106 Ibid., p. 811.

107 Ibid., p. 830.

108 Ibid., p. 775.

109 Ibid., p. 1070.

110 Ibid., p. 1113.

111 Ibid., p. 1114.

112 *Selbstkommentare*, p. 218.

113 *Joseph and His Brothers*, pp. 329–30.

114 Ibid., p. 1022.

115 Ibid., p. 1021.

116 Ibid., p. 1110. [The second sentence here is missing from Ms Lowe-Porter's version.]

117 Ibid., p. 1021. 'There is no art, no culture, not a single genuine deed (action), which *all* the forces of life have not combined to produce, the bad ones as well as the good' (*Gesammelte Werke* X, p. 609). This, like the commentary of the *Joseph* narrator, is quite against the view of Schopenhauer, who tended to the view that it would be better if the events of the world did not exist at all. The justification for blameworthy acts is provided more by the other source that already governs Aschenbach's dream, in which the Apollonian spirit collapses before Dionysus. Did not Nietzsche say that frightful talents, those regarded as inhuman, were the sole ground on

which all humanity could grow, in its impulses, acts and deeds? At least he may have said something similar; at least this is how Thomas Mann cited him in his 1921 paean to the Hermann Ungar novel *Knaben und Mörder* from which the above quote is taken.

118 *Joseph and His Brothers*, p. 1040.

119 Ibid., p. 1106.

120 Ibid., p. 1021.

121 Ibid., p. 1022.

122 Cf. Paul Scherrer and Hans Wysling, *Quellenkritische Studien zum Werk Thomas Manns*, Bern/Munich 1976, pp. 258–92. Whole chestfuls of stimuli and source material were examined in this archival rummaging. The story of Hanegiff, however, does not appear here. Wysling quotes on p. 284 how Mann wrote that he had found enlightenment from Freud on the 'culturally highly fecund morbid world of incest dread (*Inzestangst*), murder remorse (*Mördergewissensnot*), and yearning for salvation (*Erlösungsdrang*).' ('Freud's Position in the History of Modern Thought', in *Past Masters*, trans. H. T. Lowe-Porter, London 1933, p. 172 [translation modified]). Nothing in this summary of sources, however, falls under the middle term in this triad.

123 *The Holy Sinner*, trans. H. T. Lowe-Porter, London 1997, p. 25.

124 Ibid., p. 26.

125 Ibid., p. 224.

126 'I no longer thought of you / Until yesterday my sinful hands / Found the key in a fish'. See Hartmann von Aue, *Gregorius der gute Sünder*, translated from the middle and late High-German by Burkhard Kippenberg, Stuttgart 1963, p. 211.

127 *The Holy Sinner*, p. 184.

128 Ibid., p. 188.

129 Ibid., p. 226. Though hidden in its unobtrusiveness, a certain form

of address recurs in the fisherman scenes: 'Husband, husband,' his wife addresses him (p. 162) ['*Mann, Mann*' in the German], 'I don't feel right, I am not a bit comfortable about the way you acted to the wanderer!' His response is to accuse her of doting on the fool, to which she replies: 'No, husband.' Likewise with the visitation from Rome: "'Man,' replied the shorter stranger [. . .], 'man, have no concern about us' (p. 188). After his confession the cleric consoles him: 'Man, you speak after your understanding' (p. 194). There are certainly all kinds of '*Mann*' salutations with no reference to the pale confessor, so that it is impossible to decide whether this should be taken as an allusion to Thomas or not.

130 This could be read either as an extreme contraction or a one-sided compilation, but in fact it is simply a fair average, as can be checked from the collection *Selbstkommentare*. The quotations in order are from diary entry of 1 January 1946; *Selbstkommentare* pp. 206, 138, 117; *Gesammelte Werke* XI, pp. 168 and 298 ff.; and *Selbstkommentare*, p. 141.

131 *Selbstkommentare*, p. 104.

132 *The Genesis of a Novel*, p. 80.

133 Ibid., p. 144. [The second phrase quoted here is missing from Ms Lowe-Porter's translation.]

134 *Selbstkommentare*, p. 154.

135 *Doctor Faustus. The Life of the German Composer Adrian Leverkühn as Told by a Friend*, trans. H. T. Lowe-Porter, London 1992, p. 157.

136 Ibid., p. 150.

137 *Selbstkommentare*, pp. 106 ff.

138 *Doctor Faustus*, p. 143.

139 Cf. Viktor A. Oswald, 'Thomas Mann's *Doktor Faustus*: The Enigma of Frau von Tolna', in *Germanic Review 23* (1948), pp. 249–53, and *Geister und Kunst*, p. 316.

140 *Doctor Faustus*, pp. 228, 237. Cf. Michael Maar, 'Der Teufel in Palestrina', in *Literaturwissenschaftliches Jahrbuch 30* (1989), p. 218.

141 *Doctor Faustus*, p. 229.

142 Ibid., p. 253.

143 'With K[atia] on the "murders" in the book: Reisi, Annette, Preetorius, Geffcken. Bad, bad. [. . .] I paid for those "murders" with a lung operation, which was undoubtedly connected with that work' (18 July 1947).

144 *Doctor Faustus*, p. 489.

145 *Selbstkommentare*, p. 333.

146 *Doctor Faustus*, p. 290.

147 *Selbstkommentare*, p. 72. Revenge was on the part of the seduced, not of the Devil. Thomas Mann wrote to his colleague Charles Jackson of Adrian's 'deadly revenge for his defeat' (ibid., p. 88). The fairy-tale layer that he again superimposes (with Andersen's boy-killing Ice Maiden) is examined in *Geister und Kunst*, pp. 140–43.

148 Lieselotte Voss, *Die Entstehung von Thomas Manns Roman 'Doktor Faustus'*, Tübingen 1975, p. 110.

149 Michael Mann, *Schuld und Segen im Werk Thomas Manns*, p. 22. Just as it struck the Ishmaelite on his first conversation with Joseph's brothers how they repeatedly returned to the noun 'well', so it may have struck the Lübeck dignitaries on this festive occasion how frequently in his lecture Michael Mann spoke of the artist as guilty, as a highly talented sinner, even of murderers: of the 'brilliantly loathsome artist-murderer Daedalus', of Jakob Lenz, who 'perished from the illusion that he had committed the murder of his beloved', of Hoffmann's goldsmith Cardillac, who became 'an actual murderer' (p. 11). Sixteen months after this speech, Michael Mann killed himself on New Year's Eve with a mixture of alcohol and barbiturates; it has often been maintained that it was the work

on his father's diaries that drove him to this, but some scholars take a different view. Cf. Hans Wisskirchen, *Die Familie Mann*, Reinbek bei Hamburg 1999, p. 145.

150 *Selbstkommentare*, p. 302.

151 *Doctor Faustus*, p. 509.

152 Ibid., p. 511.

153 Ibid., p. 510.

154 Ibid., p. 513.

155 Ibid., p. 515.

156 Ibid., p. 468.

157 *Selbstkommentare*, p. 300.

158 *The Black Swan*, trans. W. R. Trask, Berkeley 1990, p. 139.

159 'On Schiller', in *Last Essays*, trans. Richard and Clara Winston, London 1959, p. 68. He had already at this point pronounced the nonchalant 'if you like!' in relation to his homosexuality.

160 *Confessions of Felix Krull*, p. 393.

161 Ibid., p. 398.

162 Ibid., p. 408. See also note 24 to chapter 3.

NOTES TO CHAPTER THREE

1 *Briefe an Grautoff*, p. 97.

2 If we want to arrange this into phases, we find first of all the simple – if transposed – account of a criminal act – in *Tobias Mindernickel*, in *The Wardrobe*, in *Buddenbrooks*. *Tonio Kröger* begins the second and reflexive phase, with the effort of symbolization. The events cannot be undone, but they are still burdensome, and are therefore given a supportive meaning: a meaning that breaks down time and again and has to be created anew in each work. In *The Magic Mountain*'s allegorical dream, this meaning is spelled out as a message to

humanity; this does not remove the guilt, but rather elevates it, so as to give the individual sinner breathing space beneath it. Yet this elevation also does not last, and what seemed to have healed over breaks out in new guise, as is typical of traumatic memories. The urge now becomes ever stronger to denote the act, to annul the ban by a liberating word. This would be nothing unusual for students of trauma. What is unusual – that a literary work of world stature emerges from it – does not fall in their domain.

3 *Briefe an Grautoff*, pp. 79 ff.

4 Ibid., p. 85.

5 Ibid., p. 87.

6 Ibid., pp. 90 ff.

7 Ibid., p. 94.

8 Ibid., p. 97. This 'ugly tale' combines the themes of unbridled sexual passion and deadly humiliation. At its climax, the stigmatized man is forced to dance in women's clothing.

9 Ibid., p. 90.

10 'Oh my Rome!' Thomas Mann complained back in Munich, in February 1896, 'If I could only see your pillars again! And your *people . . .*' (ibid., p. 70).

11 *Doctor Faustus*, p. 155.

12 Widespread speculation at the beginning of the twentieth century 'endowed Hungarians with the reputation of being especially inclined towards male love. Thus the very title of the anonymous novel *Teleny*, attributed to Oscar Wilde, signals that this is the story of a homosexual youth.' (Detering, *Das offene Geheimnis*, pp. 273 ff.)

13 *Doctor Faustus*, pp. 222, 400.

14 *Confessions of Felix Krull*, p. 122. The green liqueur that Rosza drinks would likely be the herbal concoction Centerbe, popular in Italy at the turn of the century.

15 *Doctor Faustus*, p. 222; *A Sketch of My Life*, p. 13.

16 *Confessions of Felix Krull*, p. 125.

17 *Gesammelte Werke* XI, p. 399.

18 *Doctor Faustus*, pp. 357–8, 403.

19 Donald A. Prater, *Thomas Mann. A Life*, Oxford 1995, p. 28.

20 Cf. *A Man and His Dog*, in *Stories of Three Decades*, London 1946, p. 456. Surreptitiously, this deals with the 'shameful horror of illegitimate and damned passion' (*Early Sorrow*, trans. H. T. Lowe-Porter, p. 526 [translation modified]). Strikingly strong words are pronounced on the occasion of the 'meeting in the open of two strange dogs', which counts among 'the most painful, thrilling and pregnant of all conceivable encounters' and is surrounded 'by a demonic and uncanny atmosphere' (*A Man and His Dog*, p. 457 [translation modified]). The snuffling dogs 'are bound to each other with some obscure and equivocal bond which may not be denied', indeed 'the same sense of guilt weighs on them both' (p. 459). The tie between canine and human activities is also drawn by an aside in *Joseph*. When Jacob kisses Rachel at the well, dogs spring up barking at them, 'as the creatures do when men, for good or evil, lay hands on each other' (*Joseph and His Brothers*, p. 151). Why this 'good or evil'?

21 Cf. diary for 5 May 1945. In the next sentence, he fortunately retracts this. 'On the other hand, it is impossible to execute a million people without imitating the methods of the Nazis.'

22 The historian Laura Schettini examined for me the daily papers *Il corriere di Napoli*, *Il Mattino*, *Il Messaggero* and *Tribuna*, as well as the police files in the Naples state archive. The striking thing about the crimes of wounding recorded there is that the victims either lie or keep silent about their assailants. The men who had to be treated for knife wounds in the Pellegrini hospital, for example, typically

maintained that while taking a walk they had intervened in a quarrel and got caught up in a fight; the women declared that someone unknown had suddenly attacked them from behind. A certain Fortuna Esposito, according to a police protocol of 14 October 1896, claimed to have 'stabbed herself out of nervousness'. The motive for this nervousness clearly had something to do with the presence of the *camorra*. As was only to be expected, the Torre Argentina quarter, where Mann stayed in Rome, was also the scene of stabbings; one would hardly expect the Roman population to stay crime-free for half a year simply because the future author of *Buddenbrooks* was living among them. None of the deeds reported or mentioned merits being examined in detail or placed in the spotlight. It is clear on the other hand that in southern Italy, at the turn of the twentieth century, conditions were different from those in Prussia, and things happened between Neapolitan heaven and Roman earth that were not recorded in police files. The failure to find such documentary evidence certainly does not imply the falsification of a hypothesis that might have been verified by such a finding.

23 *Joseph and His Brothers*, p. 1023.

24 I owe the reference to Satanism in Italy to Christian Milz and Professor Thomas Hauschild who read the German edition of this book. The latter has gathered the results of his many years' research in southern Italy into a recent book *Magie und Macht in Italien* (Gipkendorf 2003). The trail indicated by these readers is obscure but in no way absurd. All the less so, as there is a literary source that can be read as a parallel text to Mann's own subtext: *Prinz Kuckuck. Leben, Thaten, Meinungen und Höllenfahrt eines Wollüstlings*, by Mann's fellow Municher Otto Julius Bierbaum. This author, in his roman à clef published in 1906 and the following

years but today forgotten, portrayed in his protagonist the notori-
ous dandy Heymel (whom he unsuccessfully tried to blackmail
with the book), and depicted the decadent life of Europe's upper
ten thousand in the years around 1890. Bierbaum's character Felix
Henry is initiated into homosexuality by the fisherman Tiberio,
and engages his travelling companion Karl, also in love with
Tiberio, in a life-and-death struggle hushed up by the police. One
chapter expressly describes conditions in Naples, which drive Karl
with his Protestant upbringing into an outbreak of heathen sensuality. 'Here he no longer touched antique bronzes with his eyes; he
let his limbs feel living flesh. He frequented the ancient established
baths, where young attendants stalked around naked and were
ready and willing for scenes à la Petronius, for which they displayed a native talent.' This bathing temple described in such detail
also served as a contact for other establishments, as the narrator
went on to recall: 'What did it help him that here in this Naples,
where any nuance of vice could have its way, he could be a spectator of Satanic masses, at which, as Raffiano was ready to swear on
the blood of the holy Januarius, real nuns and monks took part? A
tasteless comedy! Suitable perhaps for travelling German gym-
nasium teachers, eager for a "glimpse into the abyss of Roman
decadence". Sacrilege for an entrance fee of 50 lire – how stupid!'
(*Prinz Kuckuck*, vol. II, Munich/Leipzig 1908, pp. 388 ff. and 395).
The effect that such a Black Mass might have had on the young
Thomas Mann is easy to imagine.

References to performances of this kind are even to be found in
tourist guides. A 1970 guidebook, for example, specifically mentions the street in which the visitor to Naples alighted according to
his letter to Grautoff, and the surrounding ill-famed neighbour-
hood: 'On the right side the via S. Lucia branches off, widened in

1620 after the plans of Domenico Fontana, with the demolition of fishermen's huts that formerly stood here. At the end of the 19th century, the street developed into one of the most famous and visited places of pleasure in the city. Today it forms part of the Santa Lucia quarter, full of big hotels and elegant shops . . . To the right, via S. Lucia turns into via Chiatamone, the name of which (from the Greek *platamon*) refers to the numerous grottos formed long ago at the foot of the volcanic rock of Monte Echia. Inhabited since prehistoric time, and the site of Mithratic cults, they later became a place of festive gatherings, which sometimes degenerated into scandalous orgies. The caves were accordingly destroyed by order of the Spanish viceroy Pedro de Toledo. In 1565, the embankment was surrounded with walls and became the goal of pleasure-seeking tourists of the upper classes. In the mid-18th century the first hotels were established here, including the famous "Crocelle" in what are now numbers 26 and 27, where diplomats and noble travellers particularly stayed, joined also for example by Giacomo Casanova, who sought customers here for Sara Goudar's gambling-den. On the left, at number 50, the spas and baths "al Chiatamone" were located, which used two springs of cold water [. . .] for both external and internal usage'. (Cf. Touring Club Italiano, *Napoli e dintorni*, Guide d'Italia, vol. XIX, 5th edition, Milan 1976, p. 316.)

It is not without interest that some fifteen months later, another illustrious visitor stayed at number 31, via S. Lucia – Oscar Wilde. What should hold our attention here, however, is the reference to the Mithras cult, if we recall the indications of Professor Kuckuck when he explains the game of the bloody corrida to Felix Krull. (Both their names are evocative of Bierbaum's hero Felix, known as 'Prinz Kuckuck'.) Kuckuck explains the sacrifice of the bull, described as the 'animal god' and 'horned underworld', with a 'very ancient Roman shrine whose existence testified to a deep descent from the high cult level of Christianity to the service of a divinity well disposed towards blood whose worship, through the wide popularity of the rites, almost outstripped that of the Lord Jesus as a world religion'. The next day, Felix Krull inquires yet again of Professor Kuckuck about this religion that had been so narrowly defeated. 'He could not add much, but answered that those rites had not been so completely driven from the field, for the smoking blood of a victim – the god's blood, that is – had always been a part of the pious, popular ceremonials of mankind, and he sketched a connection between the sacrament of communion and the festal, fatal drama of the day before' (*Confessions of Felix Krull*, pp. 402–3). This is an historically accurate description of the Roman cult of Mithras, an association Thomas Mann also made when he inspected San Clemente in 1953 before his Papal visit. 'The utmost antiquity, deep down to the realm of Mithras' (Diary, 1 May 1953). The suggestion of blasphemy is also found in Kuckuck's explanation. Late forms of the Mithras cult were to lead in 1910 to a scandal on Capri, where the French baron Jacques d'Adelswärd-Fersen performed homosexual black masses in the grotto of Tiberius.

The connection between modern Satanism and the Mithras cult recurs again in Anthony Powell's *A Dance to the Music of Time*, where the author describes the sect leader Trelawney, whom the narrator Nicholas Jenkins twice comes into contact with. Powell scholarship suggests that Trelawney is based on Aleister Crowley, the most famous Satanist of the twentieth century. On their second encounter in August 1939, Trelawney delivers from his sick bed a monologue interrupted by the sober replies of Mr Duport. Duport wants to know whether there will be war against Hitler.

'What do you think, Dr Trelawney?'

'What will be, must be.'

'Which means war, in my opinion,' said Duport.

'The sword of Mithras, who each year immolates the sacred bull, will ere long now flash from its scabbard.'

'You've said it.'

'The slayer of Osiris once again demands his grievous tribute of blood. The Angel of Death will ride the storm.'

> (Anthony Powell, *The Kindly Ones*, London 1997, p. 666)

In this highly comic scene, moreover, it becomes clear that the Mithras cult was always present in Crowley's obscure circle.

I plan to present the striking omnipresence of the Devil motif in Thomas Mann's work in a special study.

25 *A Sketch of My Life*, p. 38.

26 *The Fight Between Jappe and Do Escobar*, p. 339.

27 *Confessions of Felix Krull*, p. 256.

28 *Death in Venice*, p. 239.

NOTE TO TRANSLATOR'S NOTE

1 See Thomas Mann's letter to Agnes E. Meyer of 26 May 1942, in which he thanks her for reminding him of the omission of this passage, and officially agrees. *Thomas Mann / Agnes E. Meyer Briefwechsel, 1937–1955*, ed. H. R. Vaget, Frankfurt 1992, pp. 400–403.